"This well-organized and easy-to-read volume on prophecy and Jesus is a gift to the church. It concisely documents how the life and work of Christ are foretold both by the Old Testament and by the Lord himself. Along the way, *Jesus in Prophecy* retells the story of the Savior in a simple yet compelling way. Though a little book, surely it will be a big encouragement to believers as well as a useful evangelistic gift. *Jesus in Prophecy* deserves to be widely circulated; hopefully, it will also be extensively translated for the benefit of the global church."

Daniel Ebert, PhD, Director, The Christian Training and Missionary Fellowship

"'You cannot drive forward looking in the rearview mirror.' That's true of cars, true of life, and—as this book makes clear—true of Scripture. This wonderful little book, not only neatly catalogues the prophecies made about Jesus prior to his earthly ministry, but helps us understand how they now grant us confidence for traveling with him toward our eternal destinies. This is a sweet pastoral enterprise that relishes the present and future graces of the Redeemer, as well as the past predictions of his saving work."

Bryan Chapell, Pastor, Grace Presbyterian Church (PCA), Peoria, IL

"Why do people think the Bible is true? For some, the answer lies in the Bible's fulfilled prophecies—it makes predictions that came true. This book explores those prophecies by tracing the life of Jesus and detailing how he both fulfilled prophecies and made some himself. Truly, Scripture is true! Truly, Jesus was a prophet . . . and much more. Read this book to be informed, challenged, and amazed at how God knows the future . . . and holds your future in his hands."

Robert W. Yarbrough, PhD, Professor of New Testament, Covenant Seminary, St. Louis, MO

"Having pastored over fifty years (one church for forty years), I wish this book would have been available for my many years as pastor to give to those who were seeking the truth of Christianity and to new converts to Christ. *Jesus in Prophecy* will also be a blessing to mature believers as well. It not only affirms the truth of Scripture through prophecy and fulfillment, but more importantly, it reveals the truth of Jesus Christ as the promised Messiah and Redeemer of all those who trust him as their Lord and Savior. May this book have a global circulation."

Patrick J. Campbell, Retired Southern Baptist Pastor, O'Fallon, Missouri

JESUS
in PROPHECY

HOW CHRIST'S LIFE FULFILLS
BIBLICAL PREDICTIONS

VAN LEES *&* ROBERT A. PETERSON

Ichthus Publications · Apollo, Pennsylvania

Ichthus Publications
P. O. Box 707
Warrendale, PA 15095

Our goal is to provide high-quality, thought-provoking books that foster encouragement and spiritual growth. For more information regarding bulk purchases, other IP books, or our publishing services, visit us online or write to support@ichthuspublications.com.

Printed in the United States of America

ISBN: 978-1-946971-88-3 (paperback)
ISBN: 978-1-946971-84-5 (ebook)

www.ichthuspublications.com

DEDICATION

*To the brothers and sisters in Christ at
Covenant of Grace Church in St. Charles, Missouri*

Contents

Part 5 Prophecies of Jesus's Death

Part 6 Prophecies of Jesus's Resurrection

Part 7 Prophecies of Jesus's Ascension and Second Coming

ACKNOWLEDGMENTS

We gratefully acknowledge those who helped bring this book to life.

Kathi Lees and Mary Pat Peterson, our faithful wives, for their love, support, and prayers.

Adam Murrell, for believing in the Bible's message and us.

Elliott Pinegar for carefully editing the manuscript.

Geneva Durand, Ken Gontarz, Kathi Lees, Curtis Peterson, Mary Pat Peterson, Kelly Sutton, and Brian Vogel for reading the manuscript and making comments.

Carol Dempster, for compiling the topical index.

Preface

We thought a little Q&A might be helpful right here at the beginning.

How did this book come about?

I (Van) got the idea first of all from years of serving as a pastor. Through the years I've answered many basic questions from new Christians and from people inquiring about Christianity. I saw the need for an introductory book on the life of Jesus. Second, in talking to people about Jesus, I've had them ask me for one way they could know the Bible is true. Fulfilled prophecy is one of those ways. That's why we have focused on the many prophecies fulfilled in the life of Jesus.

I (Robert) got the idea for this book when noticing the materials available to worshipers on their way into the church Van pastors. Booklets, tracts, bookmarks, and information about the church are all available. But I didn't see any little books for seekers, people who don't know Jesus but want to learn more about him. This got me thinking; I spoke with Van, and the seed idea for this book was planted.

Can you tell me a little about yourself?

I (Van) was raised in an outstanding Christian home. My father and mother were good examples of how believers in Jesus should live. They have deeply impacted my life and helped make me the man I am today. Today I am pastor of the church I planted thirty-five years ago: Covenant of Grace Church in St. Charles, Missouri. I am husband to Kathi, my wife of thirty-three years. We have a son, Paul, a jazz pianist, and a daughter, Julia, a recruiter for chemists and biologists. I have made fifty trips to Ukraine over the past twenty-two years to teach in a seminary I helped to start. I now serve as president of this mission, Reformed International Theological Education.

I (Robert) was not raised in a Christian home. But I'm grateful for a father who supported the family and a devoted mother who loved and encouraged me until she passed away in 2009. I taught theology at two evangelical seminaries for thirty-five years. Today I am retired and work half-time writing and editing. Mary Pat and I have been married forty-six years and have four adult sons, Rob, Matt, Curtis, and David, our daughter-in-law, Julie, and two grandsons, Noble and Blake, whom we try to spoil.

Preface

What is your starting point in writing this?

We are evangelical Christians who have earned doctorates in theology and much experience in Christian service. But the most important things about us are that, by God's grace, we know and love the Lord and are eager for others to come to know and love him too.

Who is the audience for the book?

We wrote this small book for seekers and new Christians. Seekers are people who don't know Jesus but want answers to their questions about the Christian faith. New Christians, as the name implies, have come to know Christ but want to grow in their faith.

What is this book all about?

The book tells the greatest story ever told—the story of Jesus's life. It is also about Old Testament prophecies that predict the coming of Jesus and events in his life.

Does the book promote a denomination or church?

No, it promotes the Bible, the Word of God. Specifically, it shows how God used prophets in the Old Testament to predict many events in Jesus's life. In this way, the book demonstrates the supernatural origin of the Bible, because only God could make so many prophecies hundreds of years before he fulfilled them in Jesus.

What are the most important predictions about Jesus?

We believe the most important ones are those foretelling Jesus's death on the cross and his resurrection from the dead.

What is the format for this book?

We follow the chronological order of Jesus's life, beginning with his birth and ending with his predictions of his second coming. In between we tell of Jesus's ministry on earth, his crucifixion, his resurrection, and his ascension to heaven.

What are the purposes of this book?

Our goals are to strengthen readers' confidence in the Word of God, to help them come to know Jesus's love, and to lead them into a personal relationship with him by faith.

Introduction

What Is Prophecy, and How Is It Possible?

John first heard about Jesus in college, and he professed faith in him. Now he was middle-aged and having some doubts about his faith. John faithfully attended church and heard the Bible preached, but his doubts only increased. A friend gave him a book that criticized the Bible. It argued there were many contradictions in the Bible that could not be reconciled. This multiplied John's doubts and troubled him more. He spoke with his pastor, who gave him literature that answered many of the points argued in the book, but he still struggled with his faith.

John continued his regular practice of reading the Bible daily. One day he read Deuteronomy 18:20–22:

> The prophet who presumes to speak a word in my name that I have not commanded him to speak, or who speaks in the name of other gods, that same prophet shall die. And if you say in your heart, "How may we know the word that the LORD has not spoken?"—when a prophet speaks

in the name of the LORD, if the word does not come to pass or come true, that is a word that the LORD has not spoken; the prophet has spoken it presumptuously. You need not be afraid of him.

This gave John a direction in which he could rebuild his faith. He thought about the fact that a true prophet of God will prophesy the future with perfect accuracy. With that in mind, John began to examine some of the prophecies in the Bible, especially the Old Testament prophecies concerning Jesus. Before long he was amazed at the details of Jesus's life and ministry set forth in these prophecies. All of them were written at least four hundred years before Jesus, and many of them were written hundreds of years earlier than that. Through this he saw the supernatural character of the Bible that supported its claims to be the Word of God. He told his pastor that he was grateful for these prophecies and that Isaiah 53 was especially meaningful to him. Isaiah 53 was written around 700 B.C. and prophesied Jesus's work on the cross in great detail. Through this, John's faith was restored.

In this little book we will look at the life of Jesus and consider many of these prophetic fulfillments in his life. It is our hope that, as you read and reflect on these fulfillments, you will have the same experience John did and have either strengthened faith or initial faith in Jesus.

We begin with a treatment of prophets and their prophecies.

What Is Prophecy?

Prophecy in the Bible involves God's speaking through human beings, called prophets. God clearly distinguishes true prophets from false ones. God's true prophets speak first to their own time and sometimes make future predictions.

True and False Prophets

God told his people what to expect when they entered the Promised Land—and it was not pretty. He warned them to avoid the "abominable practices of those nations" (Deuteronomy 18:9). These involved burning children as offerings to idols and many practices designed to manipulate the so-called gods, including divination (ways to determine the mind of the gods), magic (attempts to influence events by supernatural methods), interpreting omens, casting spells, and communicating with the dead to predict the future (verses 10–13).

The Lord tells his people they are not to try to contact God or get information about the future in these ways (verse 14). Rather, they must listen to prophets God will send. Where will a prophet of God get his messages? God answers, "I will put my words in his mouth, and he shall speak to them all that I command him" (verse 18). How are the people to treat false prophets? God explains, "But the prophet who presumes to speak a word in my name that I have not commanded him to speak, or who speaks in the name of other gods, that same prophet shall die" (verse 20). How can the people tell true prophets from false ones? God answers, "When a prophet speaks in the name of the LORD, if the word does not come to pass or come true, that is a word that the LORD has not spoken; the prophet has spoken it presumptuously" (verse 22).

Prophecy Concerns the Present and the Future

When we think of prophecy, our minds race to the future. And it is true that biblical prophecy pertains to the future, but that is not the whole story. In fact, it is not the major part of the story. Primarily, prophecy pertains to the present, as the prophet brings God's message to his people living at the time. The point of prophecy is to confront people with God's life-changing message.

The prophet Isaiah, for example, makes numerous prophecies concerning the future promised Redeemer, Jesus Christ. These are among the most amazing prophecies in the Bible, and we will return to some of them later. But our point now is that they form only a small part of Isaiah's total message. The Book of Isaiah, also called the Prophecy of Isaiah, is a strong message of God's judgment against his Old Testament people Israel, whose hearts had drifted far from God and his ways. It is also a message of hope and salvation.

Sometimes prophecy speaks to both the present (forthtelling) and the future (foretelling). The prophet tells forth God's word to his contemporaries. As he does so, he sometimes foretells future events. This book mainly has to do with Old Testament prophets' foretelling or predicting events far in the future concerning the Promised One, the Messiah.

What Is Future Prophecy?

Predictions of Important Future Events

Although biblical prophets spoke more to the present than to the future, they did make future predictions. For example, God predicted that Abraham's descendants would be slaves for four hundred years (a round number) in a foreign nation and that God "will bring judgment on the nation that they serve, and afterward they shall come out with great possessions" (Genesis 15:13–14). These predictions all came true when God brought severe plagues against Egypt and delivered the Israelites from 430 years of bondage (Exodus 12). The Egyptians were so glad to see the Israelites go that they sent them on their way with gold and silver (verses 35–36). Later, when the Egyptians tried to prevent the Israelites from escaping, God divided the waters of the Red Sea so Israel could pass through, but he made the waters crash down on the Egyptians. "Thus the LORD saved Israel that day from the hand of the Egyptians, and Israel saw the Egyptians dead on the seashore" (Exodus 14:30).

God predicted that, because of its rebellion against him, the southern kingdom of Judah would be taken into captivity by the nation of Babylon for seventy years: "This whole land shall become a ruin and a waste, and these nations shall serve the king of Babylon seventy years" (Jeremiah 25:11). He also predicted that God would destroy Babylon for its sins: "Then after seventy years are completed, I will punish the king of Babylon and that nation . . . for their iniquity" (verse 12). These predictions came to pass when Babylon defeated the Israelites and took them away (2 Kings 25:1–12), and when Babylon and its king were overthrown (Daniel 5).

Predictions of the Messiah

Sometimes the prophets spoke of the future coming of the Promised One, the Messiah. Because we will deal with many of these prophecies later, here we list only a few from the Old Testament with their New Testament fulfillments. The Messiah will

- be born in Bethlehem (Micah 5:2; Matthew 2:4–6);
- be born of a virgin (Isaiah 7:14; Matthew 1:20–23);
- preach good news and freedom (Isaiah 61:1–2; Luke 4:16–21);
- die in the place of sinners (Isaiah 53:5; 1 Peter 2:24);

- rise from the dead (Psalm 16:8–11; Acts 2:24–28);
- pour out the Holy Spirit on the church (Joel 2:28–29; Acts 2:16–18).

People are sometimes surprised to learn that the Old Testament clearly predicted Jesus. Van tells such a story: "Once I met a man who said he had just converted to Judaism. In talking with him, it became apparent that he didn't know much about his nominal Christian background or Judaism. He said he would like to discuss some theological issues with me but insisted that we only use the Old Testament, since he was now a Jew. I said that would be fine and mentioned that there are things said about Jesus in the Old Testament. I then read Isaiah 53:4–6."

> Surely he has borne our griefs and carried our sorrows; yet we esteemed him stricken, smitten by God, and afflicted. But he was wounded for our transgressions; he was crushed for our iniquities; upon him was the chastisement that brought us peace, and with his stripes we are healed. All we like sheep have gone astray; we have turned—every one—to his own way; and the LORD has laid on him the iniquity of us all.

"The man objected, 'I told you I didn't want to use any passages from the New Testament.' I then pointed out that this was from the prophet Isaiah and was written a little more than 700 years before Jesus. He paused, looked thoughtful, and said, 'I'll really have to think about this more. That sure does sound like the life of Jesus.' This detailed prophecy concerning Jesus's dying on the cross as a substitute for sinners stunned him."

Why Does Future Prophecy Work?

We commonly think that prophecy works because God knows everything, including the future. This idea is correct, but fulfilled prophecy involves even more than God's supernatural knowledge. Prophecy works because God knows *and controls* the future. He orchestrates events ahead of time so that his words through the prophets come to pass. A few illustrations will help.

The Prediction that God Would Destroy Babylon

First, let's consider God's prediction through Jeremiah, cited above, that he would destroy Babylon (Jeremiah 25:12). Isaiah made similar predictions and gave the means God would use to destroy Babylon. The prophet writes in his "oracle concerning Babylon. . . . Behold, I am stirring up the Medes against them" and goes on to speak of the Medes' slaughtering the Babylonians (Isaiah 13:1, 17–18). The result? "Babylon, the glory of kingdoms, the splendor and pomp of the Chaldeans, will be like Sodom and Gomorrah when God overthrew them" (verse 19). Later we read, "I will rise up against them," declares the LORD of hosts, "and will cut off from Babylon name and remnant, descendants and posterity" (14:22).

God not only had supernatural knowledge of the future but also controlled the future by raising up the Medes, who joined the Persians, to overcome the Babylonians. Babylon surrendered to the army of Cyrus in 539 B.C.

The Prediction that Jesus Would Be Born in Bethlehem

Another example of God's predicting the future is the prophet Micah's prediction that the Messiah would be born in Bethlehem (Micah 5:2). His mother, Mary, when carrying Jesus in her womb, lived in Nazareth, fifty miles north of Bethlehem. How did God fulfill his prediction? He moved the ruler of the Roman world, Caesar Augustus, to issue a decree that all had to be registered in their hometown to prepare for taxation. Joseph, Mary's husband and Jesus's adoptive father (because Mary was a virgin when Jesus was born), took Mary and went to Bethlehem because that was his hometown. God worked in the Roman emperor, who did not know the Lord, to fulfill Micah's prophecy. He fulfilled his prediction by foretelling and controlling the future.

What Is This Book About?

This book is about two things at once. It is about Jesus's life, the greatest life ever lived. At the same time it is a book about how Jesus's life fulfilled prophecies. We will tell the story of Jesus's life, death, and resurrection and how these events fulfilled predictions made hundreds of years before by Old Testament prophets. We will include some prophecies made by Jesus himself.

Many of us find driving to new destinations easier with GPS. We think it's the same for a book, so here is a "GPS" to navigate this book. Come on a journey with us and explore:

- Prophecies of Jesus's Birth
- Prophecies of the Beginning of Jesus's Ministry
- Prophecies of the Heart of Jesus's Ministry
- Prophecies of the End of Jesus's Ministry
- Prophecies of Jesus's Death
- Prophecies of Jesus's Resurrection
- Prophecies of Jesus's Ascension and Second Coming

PART 1

Prophecies of Jesus's Birth

1

Jesus's Birth in Bethlehem

J esus's life is the most important life ever lived. We say
this because of his amazing teachings, miracles, and
casting out of demons. But we especially say it because of
the main reason he came from heaven: to die on the cross
and rise again to rescue all who trust him. Millions of
people around the world love and serve Jesus because he
loved them and gave himself for them.

Jesus's remarkable life on earth began with the fulfillment of Old Testament prophecies made hundreds of
years before he was born. In this chapter and the next,
we will look at some of those prophecies.

Why a Genealogy?

Matthew begins the story of Jesus with a long genealogy
with strange-sounding names. People sometimes ask us

why Matthew started his Gospel like this. He did so because of God's promises and prophecies to his people in the Old Testament. God called Abraham out of a pagan land called Ur and told him that the promised Redeemer would come from his line. Later in the story God made the same promise to Abraham's descendant King David. Many similar prophecies were made. While Matthew's list of names might seem strange to us, it was important to first-century Jewish people who knew about these promises and prophecies. Therefore, Matthew begins his Gospel by pointing out how "Jesus Christ" was "the son of David, the son of Abraham" (1:1), with "son" meaning "descendant."

As we look at Jesus's life, we see many fulfilled prophecies. Throughout the Old Testament, God gave increasing details about the coming Savior of his people. We find prophecies concerning his virgin birth, his birthplace, the things he would do in his earthly ministry, his betrayal by a friend for thirty pieces of silver, and, most importantly, his death and resurrection. Prophecies set forth many details of his life. These prophecies not only tell us about Jesus but also show us that the Bible is a supernatural book that comes from God. Only God could predict events hundreds of years in advance and direct history to make the prophecies come true.

Jesus Is Born of a Virgin

Matthew's genealogy leads to the story of Jesus's birth, the first miraculous event in his story. The Gospels of Matthew and Luke both tell about Jesus's virgin birth. Matthew writes:

> Now the birth of Jesus Christ took place in this way. When his mother Mary had been betrothed to Joseph, before they came together she was found to be with child from the Holy Spirit. And her husband Joseph, being a just man and unwilling to put her to shame, resolved to divorce her quietly. But as he considered these things, behold, an angel of the Lord appeared to him in a dream, saying, "Joseph, son of David, do not fear to take Mary as your wife, for that which is conceived in her is from the Holy Spirit. She will bear a son, and you shall call his name Jesus, for he will save his people from their sins." All this took place to fulfill what the Lord had spoken by the prophet: "Behold, the virgin shall conceive and bear a son, and they shall call his name Immanuel" (which means, God with us). When Joseph woke from sleep, he did as the angel of the Lord commanded him: he took his wife, but knew her not until she had given birth to a son. And he called his name Jesus. (Matthew 1:18–25)

Matthew emphasizes that Jesus's birth was a supernatural virgin birth. The child conceived in Mary was "from the Holy Spirit," not the result of sexual relations between Joseph and Mary. An angel of the Lord appeared to Joseph in a dream and assured him that the child was "from the Holy Spirit" (Matthew 1:20). Matthew points out that this fulfilled a prophecy that he quotes from Isaiah 7:14. Isaiah made this prophecy a little more than 700 years before Jesus's birth, and it was fulfilled in that virgin birth. The prophecy from Isaiah 7:14 also mentions that his name would be Immanuel, which means "God with us." This is appropriate, for God visited human beings, was "God with us," as never before. Jesus was God the Son who became a human being in order to save his people from their sins (Matthew 1:21). He would do this not as a baby but as a grown man who lived a sinless life, died in the place of rebels like us, and lived again to promise eternal life to all who trust him as Lord and Savior.

Luke gives more details about this. He tells how the angel Gabriel announced to Mary that she would conceive and give birth to Jesus. She asked how this could be, since she was a virgin. Gabriel told her, "The Holy Spirit will come upon you, and the power of the Most High will overshadow you; therefore the child to be born will be called holy—the Son of God" (Luke 1:35). Sometimes people wonder how this was possible. From a human perspective, it was not. However, when we consider God's power, this miracle is not difficult to believe. In fact, the angel Gabriel told Mary, "Nothing will be impossible for God" (verse 37).

Luke 1:32–33 also mentions a prophecy fulfilled upon Jesus's ascension. The angel Gabriel told Mary: "He will be great and will be called the Son of the Most High. And the Lord God will give to him the throne of his father David, and he will reign over the house of Jacob forever, and of his kingdom there will be no end." This refers to a prophecy given to King David that his descendant would reign forever (2 Samuel 7:12–13). Isaiah also predicts that the Messiah would be a descendant of David who would rule forever. This prophecy is often read during the Christmas season:

> For to us a child is born, to us a son is given; and the government shall be upon his shoulder, and his name shall be called Wonderful Counselor, Mighty God, Everlasting Father, Prince of Peace. Of the increase of his government and of peace there will be no end, on the throne of David and over his kingdom, to establish it and to uphold it with justice and with righteousness from this time forth and forevermore. The zeal of the LORD of hosts will do this. (Isaiah 9:6–7)

Isaiah predicts that the coming Redeemer would be both God and man. He would be "Mighty God" and "Everlasting Father" (ruler). He would also be a "child" and a "son." Jesus fulfills these prophecies because he is

God who became a man. As the foretold descendant of David, he will rule over an eternal kingdom in fulfillment of promises made to David that God would seat one of his descendants on his throne forever.

Jesus Is Born in Bethlehem

Jesus was born in Bethlehem in fulfillment of a prophecy of the Old Testament prophet Micah: "You, O Bethlehem . . . who are too little to be among the clans of Judah, from you shall come forth for me one who is to be ruler in Israel" (5:2). How did this happen, since neither Joseph nor Mary lived in that town? Rather, they both were from Nazareth, in the northern part of Israel. Luke explains:

> In those days a decree went out from Caesar Augustus that all the world should be registered. . . . And all went to be registered, each to his own town. And Joseph also went up from Galilee, from the town of Nazareth, to Judea, to the city of David, which is called Bethlehem, because he was of the house and lineage of David, to be registered with Mary, his betrothed, who was with child. (Luke 2:1–5)

This tells us why Jesus was born in Bethlehem. Joseph and Mary had to go to their ancestral city to register. God controlled the events of the Roman Empire to bring Jesus's mother Mary to the town Micah had predicted. The quotation also demonstrates that both Joseph and Mary were from the line of David, since they both had to go to Bethlehem to register. While they were there, the time came for Mary to give birth to Jesus, "and she gave birth to her firstborn son and wrapped him in cloths and laid him in a manger, because there was no place for them in the inn" (Luke 2:7).

Luke also informs us of another supernatural event at the time of Jesus's birth. In the region of Bethlehem some shepherds were out in a field, watching their sheep during the night. An angel of the Lord appeared to them, and the shepherds were extremely afraid. The angel told them not to be afraid, because he was bringing "good news of great joy that will be for all the people" (Luke 2:10). He said that "unto you is born this day in the city of David [Bethlehem] a Savior, who is Christ the Lord" (verse 11). He also told them that they would find the child wrapped in cloths and lying in a manger. As soon as the angel said this, he was surrounded by a multitude of angels who were singing and praising God, saying, "Glory to God in the highest, and on earth peace among those with whom he is pleased" (verse 14).

When the angels went away, the shepherds went to Bethlehem to see the child and the things the Lord told them. They found Mary, Joseph, and the baby lying in a manger and told everyone they met about these events (Luke 2:15–20). The angel told the shepherds amazing things about the baby: he was "Savior," "Christ," and

"Lord." "Savior" means Deliverer and is a title the Old Testament uses of God. "Christ" means the promised Jewish Messiah. "Lord" is a name the Old Testament uses hundreds of times for God. The baby would be the Deliverer of all who trust him, the promised Messiah (Christ) of Israel for the world, and God himself in human form. Matthew sums up Jesus's mission when he says that, in obedience to God, Joseph named the baby "Jesus" for, as Joseph was told, "he will save his people from their sins" (Matthew 1:21). The mission of the baby Jesus involved growing to manhood, dying, and rising from the grave to deliver all who believe in him.

So, here at the very beginning of Jesus's life, God fulfills Old Testament prophecies of his birth. These fulfillments show that the Bible is God's true Word, for only he could make predictions of the future hundreds of years ahead of time and direct history toward their fulfillment. God does not hide the identity of his Son, who became a baby. The baby is Israel's Messiah, the God-man, and the Savior of the world.

2

Jesus's Early Witnesses

Witnesses are important. We have all been witnesses at a friend's wedding. We went in support and encouragement and rejoiced to hear the pronouncement declared that the happy couple were now husband and wife "in the sight of God and these witnesses." If we were ever accused of something we did not do, we would be glad to have witnesses stand up in court under oath and speak on our behalf. We are not surprised that throughout his life Jesus had witnesses to who he was and what he had come to do. The Old Testament, God the Father, Jesus's miracles, and more testified about him. But we may well be surprised to find that baby Jesus had witnesses too! Simeon and Anna were godly, elderly people whom God allowed to see the infant Jesus before they died. They both offered praise to God and said amazing things about Jesus. This chapter examines their witness to baby Jesus.

Jesus's Circumcision

Luke 2:21 states that "at the end of eight days, when he was circumcised, he was called Jesus, the name given by the angel before he was conceived in the womb." Why was Jesus circumcised? What was the meaning of this action? In the Old Testament, God gave the people of Israel the sign of circumcision as a sign of his covenant, or promises, to them. This sign was especially to represent their faith and trust in God. It is described as a sign and a seal. Romans 4:11 describes circumcision with these terms: Abraham "received the sign of circumcision as a seal of the righteousness that he had by faith while he was still uncircumcised." In Jesus's life, Jesus fulfilled every commandment of God. We will see this repeatedly as we look at his life. He did so as a substitute for us. We also see that Joseph and Mary named the child Jesus, just as the angel had instructed both of them (Matthew 1:21; Luke 1:31).

The next event Luke tells us about also points to obedience to the law of God. Joseph and Mary took Jesus to the temple in Jerusalem to present him to the Lord (Luke 2:22–24). This was in accordance with God's law. In the Old Testament God commanded that every firstborn son belonged to him and a sacrificial offering was to be made for him (Exodus 13:11–14). This shows again the godliness of Joseph and Mary.

Simeon Testifies about Jesus

While they were in the temple, an older man named Simeon came up to them. Luke tells us about him:

> Now there was a man in Jerusalem, whose name was Simeon, and this man was righteous and devout, waiting for the consolation of Israel, and the Holy Spirit was upon him. And it had been revealed to him by the Holy Spirit that he would not see death before he had seen the Lord's Christ. (Luke 2:25–26)

Luke tells us that the Holy Spirit had given Simeon a revelation that he would not die until he saw the Messiah, the promised Redeemer. God revealed to him that the baby Jesus was this promised Redeemer. Simeon took the child in his arms, blessed God, and said:

> Lord, now you are letting your servant depart in peace, according to your word; for my eyes have seen your salvation that you have prepared in the presence of all peoples, a light for revelation to the Gentiles, and for glory to your people Israel. (Luke 2:29–32)

Astonishingly, old Simeon took a baby in his arms and told God that his eyes had seen God's salvation! Baby

Jesus would grow up to be the Savior of the world. Simeon's last phrase about Jesus's being a "light for revelation to the Gentiles" points to many Old Testament prophecies concerning salvation's going to the nations. The Old Testament focused on Israel, who showed little interest in telling other peoples about the Lord. But Isaiah had prophesied the words that Simeon used (Isaiah 42:6; 49:6; 52:10). The angels that appeared to the shepherds mentioned this same idea when they said, "Fear not, for behold, I bring you good news of great joy that will be *for all the people*" (Luke 2:10, emphasis added). In the New Testament, salvation goes beyond Israel to the whole world. People from every nation have come to know God through faith in Jesus, who grew to be a man, lived a sinless life, died for sinners, and rose again on the third day.

Simeon also prophesied about Jesus's future ministry: "And Simeon blessed them and said to Mary his mother, 'Behold, this child is appointed for the fall and rising of many in Israel, and for a sign that is opposed (and a sword will pierce through your own soul also), so that thoughts from many hearts may be revealed'" (Luke 2:34–35). "Fall" refers to those who would not believe in Jesus; "rising" refers to those who would believe in him. Simeon's words imply that Jesus would bring division among people. Some would believe in him; some would not. And there would sometimes be confrontation between the two groups, sometimes even in the same family (Matthew 10:34–36).

Simeon also predicted the initial grief Mary would feel at the time of Jesus's crucifixion: "A sword will pierce through your own soul also." These were difficult words for Jesus's mother to hear, for she was deeply grieved to see her son crucified. But of course, only a short time later God turned this grief to joy at the time of Jesus's triumphant resurrection.

Anna Testifies about Jesus

While they were in the temple, another person came up to them and said amazing things about the baby Jesus. An 84-year-old woman named Anna, who is described as a widow and a prophetess, stayed in the temple "worshiping with fasting and prayer night and day" (Luke 2:37). She approached Joseph and Mary and began giving thanks to God. She spoke about Jesus as the one promised to bring redemption to Jerusalem. She was not thinking of a political deliverance from the oppression of Rome but, just like Simeon, was speaking of how Jesus would "save his people from their sins" (Matthew 1:21).

Two Witnesses

Old Testament prophets made predictions about Jesus that came to pass. So did New Testament prophets like Simeon and Anna. God spoke through them both when they prophesied concerning the baby Jesus. They constitute two witnesses to Jesus as a baby, meeting the Old Testament requirement, repeated in the New Testament, that "every charge must be established by the evidence of two or three witnesses" (2 Corinthians 13:1; see Deuteronomy 19:15).

The Holy Spirit led Simeon and Anna to announce that the baby was "the Lord's Christ," "salvation," and "redemption" for Israel and the Gentiles. Indeed, the baby would grow to be a man and would perform the most important deeds in the history of the world. He would die on the cross to bring salvation to all who believe in him. He would rise from the dead to bring redemption to all who trust him as Lord and Savior.

3

Jesus's Visit from the Magi

The New Testament writers show that the life of Jesus from its very beginning fulfilled Old Testament prophecy. We have seen how Isaiah foretold that Jesus would have a supernatural birth and be born of a virgin. An Old Testament prophet also predicted where the Messiah was to be born. Micah wrote that "one who is to be ruler in Israel" would come forth from the small and insignificant town of Bethlehem (Micah 5:2).

We will return to the story of Jesus's life to see how Micah's prophecy fits. Matthew's Gospel provides us with further information about events in the early life of Jesus. It is good for us to introduce a few new characters to the story. Magi, or wise men, lived in the east and were students of the stars. Herod was ruler of Judea, which included Jerusalem, when Jesus was born. He was called "the great," not because of his character—he was a cruel tyrant who put his own family members to death, including his wife—but because he was a great builder who among other things rebuilt the Jewish temple in Jerusalem.

Matthew 2 tells the story of the magi from the east coming to see Jesus. Nativity scenes often show the wise men coming to Joseph, Mary, and the baby Jesus at the manger. However, verse 11 mentions that they came to the house where Joseph, Mary, and Jesus were staying. This was thus one to two years after the birth of Jesus.

The Wise Men Inquire of Herod

The wise men saw an astronomical phenomenon that they linked with the king of the Jews, and they went to the capital city of the Jews to learn more. Thus when the wise men arrived they first went to Jerusalem. They asked where they could find the newborn king of the Jews. They said they had seen his star and had come to worship him. This greatly troubled King Herod. He didn't want any rival to his position and authority. Matthew tells about this:

> Now after Jesus was born in Bethlehem of Judea in the days of Herod the king, behold, wise men from the east came to Jerusalem, saying, "Where is he who has been born king of the Jews? For we saw his star when it rose and have come to worship him." When Herod the king heard this, he

was troubled, and all Jerusalem with him. (Matthew 2:1–3)

Herod called the chief priests and scribes and asked them where the Christ was to be born. The prophet Micah's prophecy in the Old Testament about the Messiah told where he would be born. These religious leaders knew of that prophecy and quoted it to Herod: "In Bethlehem of Judea, for so it is written by the prophet: 'And you, O Bethlehem, in the land of Judah, are by no means least among the rulers of Judah; for from you shall come a ruler who will shepherd my people Israel'" (Matthew 2:4–6). Micah's prophecy concerning the birthplace of the Messiah was obviously well known. Again we see the fulfillment of an Old Testament prophecy concerning the Messiah. Of all the places in the world a baby could have been born, it was predicted that the Messiah would be born in this tiny, seemingly unimportant village near Jerusalem.

Herod called the wise men and carefully inquired of them concerning when the star appeared. He then sent them to Bethlehem with the instructions to let him know when they found the child so he could also come and worship him. But Herod had no intention of worshiping the child. He wanted to kill any potential rival to his throne.

The wise men went to Bethlehem and found Joseph, Mary, and the baby Jesus. Bethlehem was only about six miles away, almost directly south of Jerusalem, so it was not a long distance for them to go in order to find Jesus. Matthew states:

> After listening to the king, they went on their way. And behold, the star that they had seen when it rose went before them until it came to rest over the place where the child was. When they saw the star, they rejoiced exceedingly with great joy. And going into the house they saw the child with Mary his mother, and they fell down and worshiped him. Then, opening their treasures, they offered him gifts, gold and frankincense and myrrh. (Matthew 2:9–11)

The wise men were not Jews, yet here they were bowing before the baby Jesus. Their action anticipated the message of salvation going to the Gentiles in the book of Acts.

Herod Kills the Babies of Bethlehem

God warned the wise men in a dream not to return to Herod, so they went back to their country by a different route. After the wise men left, an angel of the Lord appeared to Joseph in a dream and warned him of the impending danger from Herod:

> "Rise, take the child and his mother, and flee to Egypt, and remain there until I tell you, for

Herod is about to search for the child, to destroy him." And he rose and took the child and his mother by night and departed to Egypt and remained there until the death of Herod. This was to fulfill what the Lord had spoken by the prophet, "Out of Egypt I called my son." (Matthew 2:13–15)

Here Matthew quotes Hosea 11:1. Hosea wrote these words of the nation of Israel, whom Matthew knows to be represented by the member of Israel who would rescue the nation—the Messiah Jesus.

When Herod realized the wise men had tricked him and had not come back to tell him where Jesus was, he was furious. He sent his soldiers to Bethlehem and had them kill every male child two years old or younger. Herod was cruel and vicious but was not able to defeat the plan of God to protect his Son, Jesus.

Joseph, Mary, and the baby Jesus did not have to stay in Egypt long. Herod died in 4 B.C. (Our calendars are a little off in regard to the time of the birth of Jesus.) When Herod died, an angel of the Lord appeared to Joseph in a dream and told him, "Rise, take the child and his mother and go to the land of Israel, for those who sought the child's life are dead" (Matthew 2:20). One of Herod's sons, Archelaus, succeeded him and ruled from 4 B.C. to A.D. 6. Archelaus was also a wicked man, and Joseph was again warned in a dream, so he moved his family to Galilee in northern Israel and lived in a city called Nazareth.

Lessons

We learn at least three lessons from the story of the magi. First, once again we see God fulfilling prophecies made centuries before concerning his Son, Jesus. Micah foretold that the Deliverer would be born in Bethlehem, the city of David, Israel's greatest king. Second, we learn more about Jesus's identity. The baby to be born in the city of David (Bethlehem) would one day rise from the dead as "King of kings and Lord of lords" (Revelation 19:16). As such he would rescue his people from their sins and judge his enemies. Third, we learn that, in spite of the opposition of evil people, God's plans succeed. In his providence he provided supernatural care for the infant Jesus.

PART 2

Prophecies of the Beginning of Jesus's Ministry

4

Jesus's Forerunner

The Old Testament predicts many events in Jesus's life, including his supernatural birth to the virgin Mary in the town of Bethlehem, as we have seen. Most importantly, it predicts his death and resurrection. But even before Jesus began his public ministry at age 30, God fulfilled prophecy. Two Old Testament prophets, Isaiah and Malachi, foretold that someone would come before Jesus to announce his coming. That person was John the Baptist, a strange and powerful figure, as we will see.

John the Baptist

Before the Gospels (Matthew, Mark, Luke, and John) tell the story of Jesus's public ministry, they tell about the ministry of John the Baptist. Although John appears in the New Testament, he is considered the last of the Old

Testament prophets. The Old Testament predicted his coming as a forerunner of the promised Messiah. John did two main things. First, he prepared the people's hearts for the Messiah; second, he introduced the Messiah to the people and baptized him. Luke's Gospel tells us when John began his ministry:

> During the high priesthood of Annas and Caia-phas, the word of God came to John the son of Zechariah in the wilderness. And he went into all the region around the Jordan, proclaiming a baptism of repentance for the forgiveness of sins. (Luke 3:2–3)

This places the start of John the Baptist's ministry around A.D. 26 to 29. The Jews had only one high priest at a time. The Romans had removed Annas and appointed Caiaphas, Annas's son-in-law, as high priest. While Caiaphas exercised official functions, many Jews still considered Annas to be the true high priest. When God decided to speak again to his people after a four-hundred-year absence of prophets, he did not send his word to Caiaphas or Annas. Instead he sent the word of the Lord to John. John's message was not his own but the word of God. It was a message of baptism of repentance for forgiveness of sins.

At that time, Jewish washings were of two kinds. First, if Gentiles wanted to join Israel, they would be taught the Law of God and the Old Testament. Then they would receive a ceremonial washing or baptism and be circumcised if they were male. Second, some radical Jewish groups required washings or baptisms in order to join their group. Shockingly, John called for everyone in Israel to be baptized in repentance and to prepare their hearts for the coming Messiah. All four Gospels apply Isaiah 40 to John's ministry: "As it is written in the book of the words of Isaiah the prophet, 'The voice of one crying in the wilderness: "Prepare the way of the Lord. . . . and all flesh shall see the salvation of God"'" (Luke 3:4–6, quoting Isaiah 40:3–4, 6).

John Baptizes Jesus

Jesus came to John to be baptized. John objected because he knew Jesus's identity and sinlessness. John asked, "I need to be baptized by you, and do you come to me?" (Matthew 3:14). John had a good point. Why would Jesus need to be baptized for repentance from sin? Jesus's answer is significant: they must "fulfill all righteousness" (verse 15). Then John agreed. Jesus came to be baptized to fulfill all righteousness. Part of his work was to keep all God's commands perfectly for his people, including submitting to baptism at the hands of John the Baptist.

Amazingly, when Jesus was baptized, the heavens opened and John saw the Holy Spirit in the form of a dove rest on Jesus. A voice from heaven proclaimed, "This is my beloved Son, with whom I am well pleased" (verse 17). The Father announced publicly Jesus as his Son in whom he delights. We see here the Trinity: Jesus the Son of God, the Holy Spirit as a dove, and the Father, who expressed pleasure in his beloved Son.

Various people in Israel came to John for baptism. Average people, tax collectors, and soldiers came. People began to speculate as to whether John was the promised Messiah, the Redeemer the Old Testament had promised. John emphatically denied that he was the Messiah:

> As the people were in expectation, and all were questioning in their hearts concerning John, whether he might be the Christ, John answered them all, saying, "I baptize you with water, but he who is mightier than I is coming, the strap of whose sandals I am not worthy to untie. He will baptize you with the Holy Spirit and with fire." (Luke 3:15–16)

John makes it clear that he is *not* the Promised One. In fact, John says that he is not worthy to take the role of a servant in relation to the Messiah. Untying sandals and washing feet was the job of a servant. John says that he is not qualified even to wash the Messiah's feet.

Jesus Is the Lamb of God

John's Gospel informs us that John the Baptist saw Jesus approaching and said, "Behold, the Lamb of God, who

takes away the sin of the world!" (John 1:29). This des-
ignation connects Jesus's life and ministry to the Old Testament concept of animal sacrifices for sin. God ordained
a system of worship for Israel that involved priests, a tabernacle and later a temple, altars, and animals for sacrifice.
Many sacrifices involved worshipers placing their hands
on the head of the animal and confessing their sins. The
animal was then killed as a substitute for the believing
worshipers. The animal sacrifices in the Old Testament
were prophetic as they taught that sin deserves death and
that there must be a substitute to take that penalty.

John's calling Jesus the Lamb of God is in keeping
with Old Testament prophecies that the promised Messiah would die for the sins of his people. Isaiah prophesied that the Servant of the Lord would die by the "will
of the LORD" and that his death would make an "offering
for guilt" (Isaiah 53:10). The animal sacrifices in the Old
Testament pointed forward to Jesus's death on the cross.
Jesus is the Lamb of God in two ways. First, his death
was the culmination of all the Old Testament sacrifices.
They all foretold Jesus's death. Unlike the multitude of
sacrifices performed in the Old Testament, Jesus made
one sacrifice that would put away sin for all time: he "has
appeared once for all at the end of the ages to put away
sin by the sacrifice of himself" (Hebrews 9:26).

Second, Jesus's sacrifice of himself was so powerful
that it was the basis for God's accepting the Old Testa-

ment sacrifices as atoning for the sins of believing Israelites (Hebrews 9:15). God accepted the blood of bulls and goats as an atonement for his Old Testament people's sins only because he looked ahead to Jesus's death on the cross.

Jesus is still the Lamb of God today. His death on the cross is God's only remedy for sin, the only way that God blots out sins. Only by trusting Jesus to have died in our place can we know the forgiveness of sin and gain eternal life. The Bible does not hide its main message: "God shows his love for us in that while we were still sinners, Christ died for us" (Romans 5:8). "For God so loved the world, that he gave his only Son, that whoever believes in him should not perish but have eternal life" (John 3:16).

5

Jesus's Temptations

Although every human being knows what it is to be tempted to sin, the Bible declares that "God cannot be tempted with evil, and he himself tempts no one" (James 1:13). But the Bible also plainly says that Jesus was tempted by the devil. He "in every respect has been tempted as we are, yet without sin" (Hebrews 4:15). If God cannot be tempted, and Jesus is God, how could Jesus be tempted? The answer lies in the fact that Jesus as God became a human being. As God in heaven, the Son of God could not be tempted. As the God-*man* on earth, he was tempted. Jesus's temptations were a major battle between the forces of good and evil. No Old Testament text predicted Jesus's temptations. Instead, Jesus quoted the Old Testament to defeat the evil one, who wanted to prevent Jesus from being Savior of the world.

The Holy Spirit Led Jesus into Temptation

After Jesus was baptized, the Holy Spirit led him into the desert to be tempted by the devil. This might seem like a strange occurrence in Jesus's life. We would expect him to begin his public ministry right after his baptism. However, this was an important start of his ministry for our salvation.

First John 3:8 states that Jesus came to destroy the works of the devil. The devil tempting Jesus and Jesus's victory over him are the beginnings of his victory over Satan and the Satanic kingdom. The devil tried to deter Jesus from the purpose of his coming. In this encounter with Satan, however, Jesus was victorious over him. This victory opened the door for Jesus's later plundering of the Satanic kingdom in casting out demons and freeing people from Satan's bondage (Luke 11:21–22).

The temptations point to some of the main temptations humans face. Many temptations address physical needs or drives, pride, and personal exaltation. Ultimately, these temptations were the devil's attempts to redefine Jesus's mission and to cause him to avoid the cross and empty tomb.

Satan Tempted Jesus to Turn Stones into Bread

Satan came to Jesus after he had fasted for forty days in a hostile environment in the wilderness. "The devil said to him, 'If you are the Son of God, command this stone to become bread'" (Luke 4:3). Of course, Jesus is the Son of God incarnate, but he did not use his divine power to meet his immediate physical need. Instead he answered Satan with a statement from Scripture: "It is written, 'Man shall not live by bread alone, but by every word that comes from the mouth of God'" (Luke 4:4, quoting Deuteronomy 8:3). Even though Jesus was God and man, he obeyed the Father as a man and as the representative of those who would believe in him. Just as in his baptism, he fulfilled all righteousness for us.

Satan Tempted Jesus to Test God

Satan took Jesus to the pinnacle of the temple in Jerusalem. This was probably on the southeast corner of the temple area. The top of this area was approximately 300 feet above the Kidron Valley. In this temptation, the devil also quoted Scripture, but out of context. Satan said, "If you are the Son of God, throw yourself down, for it is written, 'He will command his angels concerning you,' and 'On their hands they will bear you up, lest you strike your foot against a stone'" (Matthew 4:6). Satan quoted Psalm 91:11–12 in a way contrary to the psalm's meaning. Psalm 91 encourages God's people to trust in God. Satan attempted to replace trust with a test, casting doubt on God's faithfulness. The psalmist did not mean that the believer should try to force God's hand. This kind of miraculous display could have gained a following for Jesus but would have detracted from his mission from God to "save his people from their sins" (Matthew 1:21). Jesus again answered the devil with Scripture: "You shall not put the Lord your God to the test" (Deuteronomy 6:16). Once again Jesus used Scripture to defeat the devil's temptation.

Satan Tempted Jesus to Worship Him

The devil took Jesus to a high mountain and showed him the kingdoms of the world and their glory. He said to Jesus, "All these I will give you, if you will fall down and worship me" (Matthew 4:9). It is important to observe that it is a lie that all these kingdoms belong to Satan. While the devil is called the "ruler of this world" (John 12:31), this is true only in a limited sense. All authority belongs ultimately to God (Psalm 24:1; Daniel 4:17; Romans 13:1–4). This was a temptation to break the first of the Ten Commandments: "You shall have no other gods before me" (Exodus 20:3). This would be a terrible rebellion against the commands of God. It is also a temptation for Jesus not to accomplish the redemptive work for which he came and instead to possess a world empire at the cost of worshiping Satan. In Psalm 2:8–11 God promised to give the nations of the world to his Son, the Messiah. The devil made the same promise to Jesus, if he would commit idolatry. Jesus again answered him with Scripture: "Be gone, Satan! For it is written, 'You shall worship the Lord your God and him only shall you serve'" (Matthew 4:10).

Jesus Was Victorious over Satan

Jesus was victorious over Satan in these three temptations, and this was the beginning of Jesus's victory over the devil and his kingdom. Jesus triumphed over Satan when Jesus cast out demons from people possessed by them. The demons acknowledged Jesus's authority over them:

> Whenever the unclean spirits saw him, they fell down before him and cried out, "You are the Son of God." (Mark 3:11)

> Jesus said, "But if it is by the Spirit of God that I cast out demons, then the kingdom of God has come upon you." (Matthew 12:28)

> In the synagogue there was a man who had the spirit of an unclean demon, and he cried out with a loud voice, "Ha! What have you to do with us, Jesus of Nazareth? Have you come to destroy us? I know who you are—the Holy One of God." But Jesus rebuked him, saying, "Be silent and come out of him!" And when the demon had thrown him down in their midst, he came out of him, having done him no harm. (Luke 4:33–35)

Jesus's greatest triumph over Satan and demons took place when he died on the cross (and rose again):

Jesus said [speaking of his death], "The ruler of this world is judged." (John 16:11)

He disarmed the rulers and authorities and put them to open shame, by triumphing over them in him. (Colossians 2:15)

Since therefore the children share in flesh and blood, he himself likewise partook of the same things, that through death he might destroy the one who has the power of death, that is, the devil, and deliver all those who through fear of death were subject to lifelong slavery. (Hebrews 2:14–15)

Jesus's Victory over Satan Helps Us

What do Jesus's victories over the devil and demons have to do with us? We have enemies much stronger than we are: the devil, demons, death, and hell. None of us can defeat these enemies on our own. The very good news is that Jesus has defeated them for us. God loves us so much in Jesus that "we may have confidence for the day of judgment. . . . There is no fear in love, but perfect love casts out fear" (1 John 4:17–18). God's perfect love shown in Jesus's death drives out fear of judgment in the hearts of those who know and love Jesus. As the quotation above from Hebrews 2 says, Jesus's death destroys the devil and delivers believers from living in bondage to the fear of death. Jesus's resurrection promises believers eternal life now and resurrection from the dead when he comes again.

All in all, Jesus's victory over Satan in the temptations shows that Jesus is our Champion who loves us and defeats our enemies for us.

PART 3

Prophecies of the Heart of Jesus's Ministry

6

Jesus's Miracles

People today use the term "miracle" to describe remarkable events, especially in the world of sports. A prime example is the famous "Miracle on Ice" of 1980. This was the U.S. Olympic hockey team's amazing win over a highly-favored Russian team. As remarkable as such "miracles" are, they cannot compare to the miracles Jesus performed in his three-and-a-half-year public ministry. These were supernatural works of God. Jesus's miracles point to the facts that he is the promised Messiah and God incarnate.

When John the Baptist, imprisoned by Herod, sent followers to ask Jesus if he was "the one who is to come," Jesus told them to inform John of his miracles as evidence that he was the Messiah:

> Now when John heard in prison about the deeds
> of the Christ, he sent word by his disciples and

said to [Jesus], "Are you the one who is to come, or shall we look for another?" And Jesus answered them, "Go and tell John what you hear and see: the blind receive their sight and the lame walk, lepers are cleansed and the deaf hear, and the dead are raised up, and the poor have good news preached to them." (Matthew 11:2–5)

Jesus performed different types of miracles. We can divide these into miracles affecting nature, miracles of healing, miracles of casting out demons, and miracles of raising people from the dead. For our overview of Jesus's life we will not look at every miracle but will select examples from these four categories. In this chapter we will treat miracles of nature and healing. In the next chapter we will treat Jesus's casting out of demons, and in the following chapter Jesus's raising of Lazarus from the dead.

Jesus's Nature Miracles

Jesus Calms a Storm

After a busy day of ministry, Jesus and the disciples left a crowd of people to cross the Sea of Galilee on a boat. The distance across this lake is about eight miles. They didn't get very far when a great storm arose on the sea. This is not unusual on the Sea of Galilee. During the hot summer months the temperature on the sea can rise to around 100 degrees Fahrenheit. When the cool mountain air blows down from the areas around the lake, sudden storms easily develop and the calm waters of the sea can become extremely violent.

Mark 4:37 states, "And a great windstorm arose, and the waves were breaking into the boat, so that the boat was already filling." These experienced fishermen, who spent their lives working on this sea, were terrified by the storm. Jesus was asleep on a cushion in the stern of the boat. He was tired from a long day of ministry among the people. This showed that he was a genuine human being who needed physical rest. Jesus was apparently in a deep sleep, because the howling wind and crashing waves did not awaken him. The frightened disciples woke him and asked, "Teacher, do you not care that we are perishing?" (Mark 4:38). As soon as they cried out for help, Jesus woke up. He rebuked the wind and said to the sea, "Peace! Be still!" Immediately the wind and waves stopped and the sea was calm. The water became as smooth as glass. The disciples were amazed and filled with fear at this miracle. They asked one another, "Who then is this, that even the wind and sea obey him?"

This miracle demonstrated Jesus's majestic sovereignty over nature. The disciples might have remembered the miracle of the Israelites crossing the Red Sea (Exodus 14). They knew that God controlled the wind and the waves. Now Jesus merely spoke and these powerful forces of nature obeyed him. While sleeping in the back of the boat showed Jesus's humanity, his authority over the storm showed his deity.

Jesus Feeds the 5,000

Another example of Jesus's power over nature is the feeding of the five thousand. All four Gospels tell the story of Jesus's miraculously feeding five thousand men, not counting the women or children (see Matthew 14:13–21). When the women and children are added, the crowd may have been as large as twenty-five thousand. The Gospels tell us that this miracle occurred on the eastern shore of the Sea of Galilee in the spring of the year. Jesus had gone to this isolated place to find some privacy away from the multitudes. However, the crowds of people found him because they wanted to hear him teach and have him heal their sick. Jesus spent the day ministering to this large group of people.

At the end of the day it became apparent that the people needed food. The disciples came to Jesus and suggested that he send people to the neighboring villages to buy food. Jesus asked the disciples if they had sufficient bread for the people. Philip thought about it and calculated it would take about eight months' wages to buy enough bread for that size of crowd (John 6:7). Andrew, Simon Peter's brother, reported that a boy was present with five small barley loaves and two small fish. Of course, that amounted to nothing in terms of feeding such a large crowd of people. Nevertheless, Jesus told the disciples to have the people sit down on the grass in groups of hundreds and fifties. Jesus then took the bread and fish in his hands and blessed the food with thanksgiving to God. In doing this, he demonstrated to the people their dependence on God to supply daily needs and the necessity of giving thanks to God.

When Jesus broke the bread, a miracle of multiplication occurred. Jesus gave the bread and fish to his disciples, who distributed them among the people until all were filled. Afterward, Jesus told his disciples to gather up any that was left over, and the leftover food filled twelve baskets.

This miracle shows Jesus's care for the people. Not only did he address their spiritual needs in teaching them; he also addressed their physical needs in healing their sick and miraculously feeding them. It also demonstrated Jesus's deity. He is not only man but also God, the Creator of all things, the one who daily supplies our material needs.

Jesus's Healing Miracles

In addition to nature miracles, Jesus also performed many healing miracles. He healed many different types of maladies. A list of illnesses and conditions that he healed is impressive. Jesus did everything from curing a fever to raising people from the dead:

- Fever (Matthew 8:14–15)

- Serious, possibly fatal, illness (John 4:46–53)
- Inability to stand straight (Luke 13:11–13)
- Bleeding (Matthew 9:20–22)
- A withered hand (Matthew 12:9–13)
- A severed ear (Luke 22:50–51)
- Seizures (Matthew 17:14–18)
- Dropsy (Luke 14:2–4)
- Lameness (John 5:2–9)
- Muteness (Matthew 9:32–33)
- Deafness (Mark 7:32–35)
- Blindness (Matthew 20:30–34)
- Leprosy (Matthew 8:2–3)
- Paralysis (Matthew 9:2–9)
- Death (John 11:1–44)

The Bible sometimes summarizes Jesus's healing ministry briefly in a verse or two. Here is one such example:

> Great crowds came to him, bringing with them the lame, the blind, the crippled, the mute, and many others, and they put them at his feet, and he healed them, so that the crowd wondered, when they saw the mute speaking, the crippled healthy, the lame walking, and the blind seeing. And they glorified the God of Israel. (Matthew 15:30–31)

At other times Scripture tells stories of Jesus healing people, and these stories vary in length. One of the longest such stories is Jesus's healing of the blind man in John 9.

Healing of the Man Who Was Born Blind (John 9:1–41)

"Who Sinned, This Man or His Parents?"

Jesus and his disciples were walking in Jerusalem near the temple, where beggars would usually sit and ask for help. They passed by a well-known beggar who had been born blind. The disciples asked Jesus, "Rabbi, who sinned, this man or his parents, that he was born blind?" (John 9:2). This reflected the common belief of the day that all suffering was a direct result of sin. Jesus corrected this false belief by answering, "It was not that this man sinned, or his parents, but that the works of God might be displayed in him" (9:3). Jesus implied that he was about to work a miracle for this man and that the result would bring glory to God.

Jesus did an unusual thing in healing this blind man. He spat on the ground and made mud, which he put on the man's eyelids. There was nothing medicinal in the use of saliva or mud. In fact, it made the man even less prone to see than his congenital blindness did. Jesus wanted the man to be personally involved in showing a willingness to trust Jesus and follow his instructions. It is likely that this man who sat daily in Solomon's Colonnade in the temple area had heard Jesus teach. Now he was called upon to believe Jesus and obey what he said. Jesus told him to go wash his eyes in the Pool of Siloam, located in the southeast corner of Jerusalem.

The Blind Man Obeys Jesus

The blind man did what Jesus told him to do, going to the Pool of Siloam and washing his eyes. When he did so, his eyes were healed and he could see perfectly. Imagine the emotions he would have felt. He had heard people speak of the blue sky or the green grass, but since he was born blind he had had no concept of what that meant. Now he was looking at the sky, the grass, and the things around him and for the first time in his life was seeing his surroundings. He rushed home to see his father and mother and tell them what had happened.

> The neighbors and those who had seen him before as a beggar were saying, "Is this not the man who used to sit and beg?" Some said, "It is he." Others said, "No, but he is like him." He kept saying, "I am the man." So they said to him, "Then how were your eyes opened?" (John 9:8–10)

The man told them of how Jesus had healed him. This started a controversy. The neighbors brought him to the Pharisees (the religious leaders) so they could make an evaluation concerning this amazing event.

"Though I Was Blind, Now I See"

The Pharisees asked the man how his blindness had been healed. He told them of how Jesus made the mud, applied it to his eyes, and told him to wash it off in the Pool of Siloam. The Pharisees did not react with joy or glorify God for this great miracle. It was the Sabbath when Jesus healed this man, and these religiously-strict Pharisees concluded that Jesus had sinned in three ways in performing this miracle: he made mud, put it on the man's eyes, and healed him. They saw this as working on the Sabbath Day, which was supposed to be a day of rest. Therefore, since Jesus was in violation of the Law, he was a sinner and could not be from God. However, some of the Pharisees disagreed and asked, "How can a man who is a sinner do such signs?" (John 9:16). They argued among themselves, so they asked the healed man for his opinion concerning Jesus. He quickly answered, "He is a prophet" (John 9:17).

Now they began to question whether the man had really been blind, asking his parents if this was really their son who was born blind. They affirmed that it was truly their son who was born blind, but they did not want to comment on how he had been healed. They were noncommittal because they knew the Pharisees had proclaimed that anyone who confessed Jesus to be the Christ (the Messiah) would be put out the synagogue. The parents pleaded ignorance and told the leaders to ask their son how it had happened.

The man who was healed was not hesitant to affirm that Jesus had healed him. Apparently at this point the Pharisees had reached the conclusion that Jesus was truly an evil person. They told the man, "Give glory to God; we know that this man is a sinner" (John 9:24). This was a way of saying, "Tell the truth," and the truth they wanted the man to tell was that Jesus was a sinner. The man who was healed gave a wise answer: "Whether he is a sinner I do not know. One thing I do know, that though I was blind, now I see" (John 9:25). Upon this answer, the Pharisees tried to go over the same ground again, asking him to tell once more how he had been healed.

The healed man refused to be a part of this and told them he had already explained it to them, and there was no need to do so again. He even asked them if they wanted to become Jesus's disciples. They replied harshly: "They reviled him, saying, 'You are his disciple, but we are disciples of Moses. We know that God has spoken to Moses, but as for this man, we do not know where he comes from'" (John 9:28–29). The former blind man replied in astonishment,

> "Why, this is an amazing thing! You do not know where he comes from, and yet he opened my eyes. We know that God does not listen to sinners, but if anyone is a worshiper of God and does his will, God listens to him. Never since the world began has it been heard that anyone opened the eyes of

a man born blind. If this man were not from God, he could do nothing." (9:30–33)

The former blind man was right. Many miracles were performed in the Old Testament, but never did someone born blind receive his or her sight. The healed man pointed out the simple fact that once he was blind but now could see. This incredible miracle points to Jesus's being not an evil person or a charlatan but the Son of God.

The Jewish Leaders Oppose Jesus

This enraged the Pharisees. They held that the healed man was a sinner because he had been born blind. They indignantly asked, who was he to instruct them? They hated Jesus so much that they did not remember Isaiah's prophecies that the Messiah would restore the sight to the blind:

> Behold my servant, whom I uphold, my chosen, in whom my soul delights; I have put my Spirit upon him; he will bring forth justice to the nations. . . . Thus says God, the LORD, who created the heavens and stretched them out, who spread out the earth and what comes from it, who gives breath to the people on it and spirit to those who walk in it: "I am the Lord; I have called you in righteousness; I will take you by the hand and keep you; I will give you as a covenant for the

people, a light for the nations, to open the eyes
that are blind, to bring out the prisoners from the
dungeon, from the prison those who sit in darkness. (Isaiah 42:1, 5–7)

The Pharisees expelled the formerly blind man from the
synagogue.

"Do You Believe in the Son of Man?"

Jesus heard that the man had been cast out. He found
him and asked, "Do you believe in the Son of Man?" The
blind man had never seen Jesus; he had only heard him.
He asked him who the Son of Man was so that he could
believe in him. Jesus said to him, "You have seen him,
and it is he who is speaking to you" (John 9:35–37).
Upon hearing this the man said, "'Lord, I believe,' and
he worshiped him" (9:38). The Pharisees, who claimed
to have great spiritual sight, did not see the truth of who
Jesus was. Ironically, a formerly blind man could see who
Jesus was better than the leaders of Israel could! The man
who was born blind saw clearly who Jesus was, and he
worshiped him.

In this healing miracle we see the fulfillment of prophecy, substantiating the Bible's claim to be the Word of
God. Only God could predict the future and bring it to
pass without mistake. We also see Jesus's divine power.
Why was he able to perform nature miracles, including
calming a storm and feeding over five thousand men, and

various healings listed at the beginning of this chapter? Because he is the Son of God and Savior of the world. We also see the spiritual blindness of the religious leaders, who claimed to have great spiritual insight. Finally, we see Jesus's giving spiritual as well as physical sight to the man who had been born blind.

7

Jesus's Exorcisms

Setting "at liberty those who are oppressed." At the beginning of his ministry Jesus stated that this was part of what he had come to accomplish. As we saw in chapter 6, Jesus read these words from Isaiah at his home synagogue in Nazareth (Luke 4:18). Then he announced that these words had found fulfillment in him. The Holy Spirit anointed Jesus to cast demons out of people who were oppressed by them. In casting out demons, Jesus "set at liberty those who are oppressed." There are numerous examples of this in the Gospels. We will consider one of the more dramatic ones.

Jesus Frees Demon-possessed Men

Jesus had calmed a great storm that had frightened his fishermen disciples because the waves had been swamping their boat. Jesus had merely spoken to the winds and

the sea, and they obeyed him! As a result the sea immediately grew calm. At this the disciples were amazed and
wondered what sort of person he was (Matthew 8:27).

No One Could Bind Him Anymore

After this, Jesus and his disciples sailed in the boat to the
southeast side of the Sea of Galilee. This was a Gentile
region in the area of a town named Gadara. As Jesus was
getting out of the boat, a demon-possessed man came up
to him. Matthew mentions two men, while Mark and
Luke speak only of one. It is possible that one man did
the speaking for both and that Mark and Luke therefore
focus on him. These men were not only mentally ill. They
had supernatural strength and would break chains when
people bound them. Mark informs us of the situation of
one of them:

> He lived among the tombs. And no one could
> bind him anymore, not even with a chain, for he
> had often been bound with shackles and chains,
> but he wrenched the chains apart, and he broke
> the shackles in pieces. No one had the strength to
> subdue him. Night and day among the tombs and
> on the mountains he was always crying out and
> cutting himself with stones. (Mark 5:3–5)

Apparently these men used to live in one of the nearby
towns but now lived among the tombs. This probably
refers to caves used as burial chambers in the side of cliffs.

People could hear them screaming during the day and night. Their screams would echo from cavern to cavern and along the rocky shore. We can imagine the fear this would generate among the people who lived in that area. Matthew tells us that people would go out of their way to avoid that area because of the demon-possessed men (Matthew 8:28). The destructive nature of the demons is also seen in the men gashing themselves with the sharp edges of stones. When people tried to subdue them and bind them, they broke the chains with which they had been bound. This is a terrifying picture, like something out of a modern horror movie. However, it is not fiction but a true situation showing why Jesus described Satan as the one who comes "only to steal and kill and destroy" (John 10:10).

The Demons Know Jesus's Identity

The one speaking for the demon-possessed men came up to Jesus, "and when he saw Jesus from afar, he ran and fell down before him. And crying out with a loud voice, he said, 'What have you to do with me, Jesus, Son of the Most High God? I adjure you by God, do not torment me'" (Mark 5:6–7). Unbelieving people often deny that Jesus is God, but these demons did not; they knew who he was. As Jesus commanded them to come out of the men, the demons begged Jesus not to torment them. Matthew adds that the demons asked him not to torment them before the appointed time (Matthew 8:29). A day of final judgment is coming for both demons and unbelieving human beings.

The demons recognized who Jesus was and his authority over them. Jesus then commanded the demon to tell him his name. The demons replied, "My name is Legion, for we are many" (Mark 5:9). We are now given insight into how severe was the demonic possession of these men. Not merely one demon, but many demons possessed them. In the Roman army, a legion was a force of at least six thousand men. While the name should not be taken literally to mean six thousand demons, it does indicate a large number. Again, the demons begged Jesus not to send them out of the area.

A Large Herd of Pigs

A large herd of pigs was feeding on a nearby hillside, and the demons asked Jesus to send them into the pigs. Jesus gave them permission, and the demons came out of the men and entered the pigs. The herd, which numbered about two thousand, rushed down the steep bank into the sea and drowned (Mark 5:13). The herdsmen fled and told the people in the nearby city what had happened. There is a mysterious element as to why the demons wanted to go into the pigs and why Jesus allowed them to do so. It is possible that this reflected the demons' hatred for God and all of his creation as well as their desire to create animosity against Jesus in that community. Also, the appointed time for the full judgment of the demons had not yet come.

The people came out of the city to Jesus and saw the once-demon-possessed men sitting there clothed and in their right minds. Now these men were not a source of terror but were completely normal. The response of the people was fear, and they began to beg Jesus to depart from their region (Mark 5:15–17). They were afraid of the supernatural power Jesus demonstrated in casting out the demons. It is also possible that their real values were exposed in the loss of the herd of pigs. They cared more about the pigs and financial gain than they did about the two men.

As Jesus was getting into the boat to leave, the men wanted to go with him. However, Jesus did not permit them but instead spoke to the one who had made the request: "Go home to your friends and tell them how much the Lord has done for you, and how he has had mercy on you" (Mark 5:19). Jesus is the one who had set the men free from the demons, but this deed is described as an action of the Lord. This again affirms the deity of Jesus. The people had asked Jesus to leave, but he left a witness to himself in the community. The men who had been delivered from the demons were now missionaries to their community, and they could speak from experience concerning the power and mercy of Jesus.

Jesus Still Sets at Liberty the Oppressed

In casting out these demons, Jesus did what he had said he had come to do—he "set at liberty those who are oppressed." The good news is that Jesus continues to deliver the oppressed today. Although at his name demons are still routed, much more frequently Jesus frees those oppressed by sin and guilt. We cannot wash away our sins on our own. It is very good news, then, that God promises, "Though your sins are like scarlet, they shall be as white as snow; though they are red like crimson, they shall become like wool" (Isaiah 1:18). Only God can deliver us from our sins, and this is exactly what Jesus did. He died for our sins and arose conquering our enemies, including Satan and demons. If we trust Christ as Lord and Savior, he will forgive our sins and set us at liberty too.

This is exactly what Ken found out. Here is his story. From the world's perspective, Ken's life was going great. He was thirty years old and single, had a great job with a Fortune 100 computer company, bought his first house in an upper-middle-class subdivision, and indulged in many of the pleasures the world had to offer. As part of his job providing worldwide technical support for a particular product, he would occasionally go to the company's corporate headquarters to receive training on new releases. On one particular training session, a remarkable life-changing confrontation took place. John, one of the product's developers, befriended Ken. After the first day of training, they discovered they enjoyed playing chess and wound up playing at their hotel's lobby that evening.

All was going well, the conversation was cordial, and they were having fun playing chess when Ken blurted out, "Jesus Christ, what a stupid move that was!" At once the demeanor of John became confrontational and deadly serious. Putting his finger in Ken's face, he sternly said, "Don't you ever use that name in that manner again. I know that man. Should the day ever come when you want to know about that man, give me a call." Ken was so taken aback that for a moment he thought of grabbing his newfound friend's beard and popping him right in the face. However, that would have been a mistake, a bad mistake. As it turned out, John held a black belt in judo in the Air Force and was on its judo team. Things settled down and the chess continued, as did the new-found friendship. In addition to chess, the two had other things in common as well, such as racquetball and similar backgrounds, including growing up in the same city.

Fast-forward several months. Ken's life was on cruise control and couldn't be going any better—or so he thought. It was Monday night. He was in his living room with his feet up on the coffee table, reading the sports page with his golden retriever by his side when—bam!— he was suddenly cast into blackness. He was fully conscious but unable to see. "What's happening?" he cried out as he dropped to his knees. Scared, really scared, he remembered appealing to God, saying, "God, I don't know what's going on, I don't know if you exist but if you do, please help me!"

The intense moments of sheer terror seemed like an eternity, but upon examination nothing was medically wrong, and Ken's eyesight came back on its own. His thoughts turned inward, and for some reason he remembered the offer of his new friend: "Should the day ever come when you want to know about that man, call me." The time could not have been any more right. The next day Ken called John: "John, this is Ken. Remember that night while playing chess when you offered . . . ?" John interrupted, "Of course, I do. Come on over. Would love to talk."

They engaged in quite a dialogue. For hours, Ken asked question upon question. "What do you think about this? What do you think about that?" John's response to every question was the same: "It doesn't matter what I think. Let's see what the Word of God says." Skillfully, John answered every one of Ken's questions directly from the Bible. Then the moment came when John quoted Romans 14:11–12: "For it is written, 'As I live, says the Lord, every knee shall bow to me, and every tongue shall confess to God.' So then each of us will give an account of himself to God."

John noted later that it was like scales dropped from Ken's eyes. The light had penetrated Ken's heart, and he knew that night the certainty that he would stand before God and give an account of himself and that he therefore needed a Savior. He needed Jesus! He prayed, expressing his faith in Jesus as his Savior. John gave Ken a Bible. Every morning before work and every night after work for the next year Ken voraciously read the Bible. He started attending church with John and his family. And God turned his life around 180 degrees, from sin to obedience to Christ.

Three years later John was Ken's best man in his wedding.

8

Jesus's Raising of Lazarus

We have many enemies: the world as a system against God, our propensity to sin, Satan, demons, and hell. Scripture says that the last enemy is death, which God will one day destroy (1 Corinthians 15:26). This will occur when God raises believers' bodies to eternal life with God on the new earth. In the meantime, death is an enemy of all human beings. Christians will be raised to eternal life because Jesus died and rose from the dead. And during his earthly ministry he pointed to the final resurrection when he resuscitated three people from death.

Jesus Overturns Death

While imprisoned, John the Baptist sent to inquire of Jesus as to whether he was truly the Messiah. Jesus answered, "Go and tell John what you hear and see: the blind receive their sight and the lame walk, lepers are cleansed and the deaf hear, and the dead are raised up, and the poor have good news preached to them" (Matthew 11:4–5, quoting Isaiah 35:5–6). Although there is not a direct Old Testament prophecy that speaks of the Messiah's raising the dead, prophecies do address his healing the brokenhearted and setting free those in bondage, both of which are caused by death. Isaiah 61:1–3 proclaims:

> The Spirit of the Lord GOD is upon me, because the LORD has anointed me to bring good news to the poor; he has sent me to bind up the broken-hearted, to proclaim liberty to the captives, and the opening of the prison to those who are bound; to proclaim the year of the LORD's favor, and the day of vengeance of our God; to comfort all who mourn; to grant to those who mourn in Zion—to give them a beautiful headdress instead of ashes, the oil of gladness instead of mourning, the garment of praise instead of a faint spirit; that they may be called oaks of righteousness, the planting of the LORD, that he may be glorified.

Perhaps the most dramatic of Jesus's miracles were the three times he raised the dead. He raised a widow's only son (Luke 7:11–17), a little girl who had just died (Matthew 9:23–26), and Lazarus, the brother of Mary and Martha, after he had been dead four days (John 11:1–44). In raising the dead, Jesus healed the brokenhearted, comforted those who mourn, gave hope concerning the bondage of death, and proclaimed the year of the Lord's favor. Jesus quoted this passage and applied it to himself at the beginning of his ministry (Luke 4:16–21).

Mary and Martha, two sisters, and Lazarus, their brother, lived in the village of Bethany, about two miles east of Jerusalem. They had developed a friendship with Jesus; when he was in that area he would visit and stay with them. Near the end of Jesus's earthly ministry, he and his disciples were staying on the east side of the Jordan River, where they were safe from attacks from Jewish religious leaders. Mary and Martha sent an urgent message to Jesus concerning Lazarus: "Lord, he whom you love is ill" (John 11:3). Their expectation was that Jesus would come immediately and heal their brother. However, Jesus delayed going, waiting two days. He told the disciples that Lazarus's sickness was so that "God may be glorified through it." This remark pointed toward an astounding miracle Jesus would perform. During the time he waited, Lazarus died.

When Jesus arrived in Bethany, he found that Lazarus had been dead for four days and was already in the tomb. However, this was not a surprise to Jesus. He had told his disciples that Lazarus had died and that he was going to awaken him (John 11:11–15). Since Bethany was close to Jerusalem, many people came to console Mary and Martha.

Jesus Meets Martha

Martha met Jesus as he approached their home, but Mary, her sister, stayed in the house, grieving her brother's death. When Martha met Jesus she said, "Lord, if you had been here, my brother would not have died. But even now I know that whatever you ask from God, God will give you" (John 11:21–22). Perhaps throughout their brother's illness Mary and Martha had made the statement to each other that, if Jesus were only there, he could have healed Lazarus. Martha's statement was one not of reproach but of grief. She also expressed great faith in Jesus by stating that whatever he asked of God would be given to him. The hope that Jesus could raise Lazarus from the dead was in the mind of Martha. Jesus told her, "Your brother will rise again." Martha, as a Jewish woman who knew the Old Testament, knew the prophecies of a resurrection on the last day. She replied, "I know that he will rise again in the resurrection on the last day" (John 11:23–24).

Jesus then made a profound statement: "I am the resurrection and the life. Whoever believes in me, though he die, yet shall he live, and everyone who lives and believes in me shall never die. Do you believe this?" (John 11:25–26). Jesus's statement means that everyone who believes in him has already received eternal life, a life that can ultimately never be taken away. Martha replied with a statement of great faith in Jesus: "Yes, Lord; I believe that you are the Christ, the Son of God, who is coming into the world" (11:27). She confessed that she believed Jesus to be the Christ, the Messiah promised throughout the Old Testament. It is noteworthy that Jesus received Martha's confession that he was the Messiah and the Son of God.

Jesus Meets Mary

Martha went and got her sister, Mary. When Mary came to Jesus, she repeated what Martha had said: "Lord, if you had been here, my brother would not have died" (John 11:32). This suggests that throughout Lazarus's illness they must have been saying, "If only Jesus were here." Jesus was very sympathetic to the grief of Mary and Martha: "When Jesus saw her weeping, and the Jews who had come with her also weeping, he was deeply moved in his spirit and greatly troubled. And he said, 'Where have you laid him?' They said to him, 'Lord, come and see.' Jesus wept" (John 11:33–35). The Jews who witnessed Jesus's response to Lazarus's death were divided in their interpretation of Jesus's tears. Some said, "See how he loved him!" (John 11:36). Others asked why this man who had opened the eyes of the blind had not prevented Lazarus from dying.

Jesus Raises Lazarus

The cave that served as a tomb for Lazarus had a stone across its entrance. Jesus told the people to remove the stone. Martha immediately reacted and said, "Lord, by this time there will be an odor, for he has been dead four days" (John 11:39). Martha knew that the body was already starting to decompose. Jesus gently reminded her that, if she believed, she would see the glory of God. The stone was removed. Jesus then looked up to heaven and prayed a prayer of thanksgiving to God the Father. After doing so he cried out in a loud voice, "Lazarus, come out." Lazarus came out of the tomb with his hands and feet bound in the linen burial strips and his face wrapped with a cloth. Jesus instructed others to unbind him and let him go. Jesus performed a tremendous miracle. A man who had been dead for four days was raised to life.

Responses to This Miracle

Many of the prominent Jews saw what Jesus did and believed in him. However, some went and told the Pharisees, who did not respond in faith. Instead, the chief priests and Pharisees gathered the council and decided that they must kill Lazarus as well as Jesus since many were believing in Jesus because of this miracle (John 11:45–53; 12:9–11). How sin blinds our eyes! Apart from God's grace, people in sin do not believe even if they see great miracles.

Once again we see fulfilled prophecy in Jesus's life, this time as a prelude to his future final victory over our enemy death. Death has touched all of us in various ways: the death of parents, siblings, children, or friends. Those who believe in Jesus really grieve those deaths, but they don't grieve as those who have no hope. People who believe in Jesus have a hope based on the promises of God. The Bible teaches that the souls of all who believe in Jesus immediately go to heaven and are with him at their death. And then one day God will resurrect their bodies without flaws to enjoy eternal life with God. This is his final and glorious victory over death. This will be a life without sin, conflict, or sorrow of any kind. In addition, even as Jesus comforted the brokenhearted in returning Lazarus to his sisters, believers in Jesus have comfort in this life in knowing that Jesus is always with them. And—as surely as Jesus died for our sins and arose—believers in him have hope that they are truly forgiven and accepted by God.

Jesus Triumphs over Death

Andrew was only fifteen years old. He was academically gifted and earned perfect scores on the ACT and SAT tests. However, the most important thing in his life was his faith in Jesus and his desire to live for God's glory. At one point in life he experienced pain in his leg and received a difficult diagnosis. He learned he had a type of bone cancer known as osteosarcoma. Over the next six years he received the best medical treatment available, but the disease progressed. During this time his academic ability was recognized and he was named a Presidential Scholar. He was too sick to travel to Washington, D.C., to receive the award, but President George W. Bush landed Air Force One in St. Louis and presented the award to him.

When he was in hospice and knew that his life on this earth was about over, Andrew invited friends who did not know Jesus as their Savior to his bedside and presented the good news of Jesus's work of salvation to them. Finally the disease ran it course, and Andrew went home to his Lord. His parents grieved over the loss of their only son but knew that Andrew's life was not really over. He was now in heaven with Jesus, just as he had promised those who believe in Jesus. His parents grieved, but not as those who have no hope. His father said, "Heaven is now a little sweeter place to me." Jesus's promise when speaking with Martha continues to comfort Andrew's parents and friends: "I am the resurrection and the life. Whoever believes in me, though he die, yet shall he live" (John 11:25). Even when believers' bodies die, their souls immediately are in God's presence and enjoy a perfect existence with him.

There is even more to the story. We can think of the Christian life in terms of "good, better, and best." People who believe in Jesus know that they are forgiven for all their sins. This is the real answer to real guilt. Believers know they are adopted into God's family and have his fatherly care. This is *good*. When a Christian dies, it is *better*. The apostle Paul, in speaking about his death, said, "My desire is to depart and be with Christ, for that is far better" (Philippians 1:23). The *best* is the future resurrection when Jesus returns. Believers will be resurrected, with soul and body reunited. They will have powerful and glorious bodies that will never again be weak, get sick, experience pain, or die. This Christian hope not only comforts us in times of death and grief but also sets before us a glorious future as the redeemed people of God.

PART 4

Prophecies of the End of Jesus's Ministry

9

Jesus's Predictions of His Death and Resurrection

Jesus was not only the subject of prophecy but also a prophet himself. Most of this book shows how Jesus's life fulfills Old Testament predictions made hundreds of years before. It is also vital to know that Jesus *made* many predictions. He made predictions about the Jewish people, the Gentiles, the temple, his disciples, the coming of the Holy Spirit, and events following his second coming. His most important predictions were of his death and resurrection. We will focus on these, because Jesus's death and resurrection are the most important events in the history of the world.

Jesus Is a Prophet

The writer to the Hebrews tells us that Jesus was a prophet. In fact, he presents Jesus as the supreme prophet when contrasting him with Old Testament prophets: "Long ago, at many times and in many ways, God spoke to our fathers by the prophets, but in these last days [God] has spoken to us by his Son" (Hebrews 1:1–2). God spoke through the Old Testament prophets in various ways, but when Jesus came God focused his revelation and spoke "by his Son." In this way all of the New Testament is revelation about and from Jesus. He fulfills the Old Testament, and he sent the Holy Spirit to his apostles so they could write the New Testament.

Jesus Is Like and Unlike Other Prophets

Jesus was like Old Testament prophets in many ways. They spoke God's Word to the people. They confronted the people with the Lord's claims and called them to be faithful to the covenant. They rebuked the people for disobeying God and not listening to his prophets. Jesus did these same things. He spoke for God (Matthew 4:23) and brought God's claims to his hearers (4:17). He summoned them to covenant faithfulness (5:16) and rebuked them for their unbelief and disobedience to God (Matthew 23).

Jesus was a prophet and more than a prophet. He was unique. To which of the prophets did God ever speak the words that he said to Jesus at his baptism: "This is my beloved Son, with whom I am well pleased" (Matthew 3:17)? What prophet besides Jesus claimed, "Heaven and earth will pass away, but my words will not pass away" (24:35)? What prophet could say with Jesus, "I am the way, and the truth, and the life. No one comes to the Father except through me" (John 14:6)? To ask these questions is to answer them. Jesus is utterly unique, and it is good for us to probe his uniqueness further.

Jesus Is Like No Other

The fundamental difference between Jesus and other prophets has to do with who he was.

First, he was sinless. Every other prophet was a sinner who needed God's forgiveness. Not so Jesus. Unlike the rest of us, Jesus never sinned. Paul says that Jesus "knew no sin" (2 Corinthians 5:21). The writer to the Hebrews says that Jesus "in every respect has been tempted as we are, yet without sin" (Hebrews 4:15). Peter adds, "He committed no sin" (1 Peter 2:22, 23). Indeed, he is "Jesus Christ the righteous" (1 John 2:1), and "in him there is no sin" (3:5).

Second, Jesus is unlike every other prophet in his identity because he is God. He, the eternal Son of God, left heaven to become a man (John 1:14). He is God in his very essence (Hebrews 1:3). The titles given to him show that he is God, for he is called "God" (John 1:1; 20:28; Titus 2:13; Hebrews 1:8), "the Lord" (Hebrews 1:10), and "the Son of God" in a manner that makes him equal to God (John 5:18).

In addition, Jesus does the works that only God can do, such as creation (John 1:3) and judgment (John 5:22). Jesus's most important work is rescuing us sinners. Only God can save sinners, and that is what Jesus does! He dies to save them (1 Corinthians 15:3–4), rises from the dead to save them (John 14:19), will raise believers from the dead (5:27–29), and invites them into his eternal kingdom (Matthew 25:34).

Good men and angels reject worship (Acts 14:11–15; Revelation 22:8–9), but Jesus receives it (John 9:38; Hebrews 1:6). Further, because he is the God-man, only Jesus could make amazing promises like this: "Truly, truly, I say to you, whoever hears my word and believes him who sent me has eternal life. He does not come into judgment, but has passed from death to life" (John 5:24). Jesus is like no other prophet because he is a sinless man and God himself!

Jesus Predicted His Death and Resurrection

Jesus taught his contemporaries and also foretold the future. He predicted the Jews' rejection of their Messiah (Matthew 23:37–38) and the temple's destruction (24:2). Jesus prophesied that one of his disciples would betray him (26:20–25). He foretold his return (24:30–

31), the last judgment (25:31–36), and the final kingdom of God (19:28). On three occasions Jesus foretold
his arrest, death, and resurrection.

> From that time Jesus began to show his disciples
> that he must go to Jerusalem and suffer many
> things from the elders and chief priests and
> scribes, and be killed, and on the third day be
> raised. (Matthew 16:21; see also Mark 8:31; Luke
> 9:22)

> As they were gathering in Galilee, Jesus said to
> them, "The Son of Man is about to be delivered
> into the hands of men, and they will kill him, and
> he will be raised on the third day." (Matthew
> 17:22–23; see also Mark 9:31; Luke 9:44)

> See, we are going up to Jerusalem. And the Son
> of Man will be delivered over to the chief priests
> and scribes, and they will condemn him to
> death and deliver him over to the Gentiles to be
> mocked and flogged and crucified, and he will be
> raised on the third day. (Matthew 20:18–19; see
> also Mark 10:33–34; Luke 18:32–33)

It is helpful to view the details of the passages above
from the Gospel of Mark in chart form.

Mark 8:31	Mark 9:31	Mark 10:33–34
Suffering		
	Delivered to Jews	Delivered to Jews
Rejected by Jews		

Mark 8:31	Mark 9:31	Mark 10:33–34
		Condemned
		Delivered to Gentiles
		Mocked
		Flogged
Killed	Killed	Killed
Will Rise	Will Rise	Will Rise

Jesus was the great prophet of God. There was never another like him. He foretold that he would suffer much and be delivered to the Jewish authorities, who would reject and condemn him (by trial). He predicted that the Jews would deliver him over to Gentiles (for trial), who would mock him, flog (beat) him, and put him to death. He also foretold that he would rise from the dead. Jesus thus foretold his death and resurrection three times.

Jesus's Message Is for Us Too

We have focused attention on Jesus's death and resurrection for a number of reasons. First, they were his most important predictions. Second, they are the most important events in the history of the world. Third, they form the heart of God's good news, the gospel of salvation. Speaking of himself, Jesus said, "Even the Son of Man came not to be served but to serve, and to give his life as a ransom for many" (Mark 10:45).

The Bible describes our situation before we came to know Jesus in this way: we were in bondage to sin, Satan, and self. We needed redemption, deliverance from these cruel masters. And that is just what God provided through his Son. Jesus gave himself to die in our place as a ransom. His death is the ransom price given to redeem (rescue) all who believe in him.

Jesus is not only a prophet; he is also a priest. As such he sacrificed himself on the cross to rescue human beings. Hebrews says that Jesus's death secured an "eternal redemption" (Hebrews 9:12) and "put away sin by the sacrifice of himself" (9:26). Indeed, "by a single offering he has perfected for all time" those who trust him (10:14). We invite readers to turn from efforts to make themselves right with God and to trust Jesus's death and resurrection as the only way to God.

10

Jesus's Triumphal Entry into Jerusalem

R epeatedly throughout his ministry, Jesus received two responses to his words and deeds. After Jesus taught the words that the Father gave him or did unheard-of miracles, many believed in him. However, many who heard the same words and saw the same miracles rejected him.

Conflicting Responses to Jesus

We see this pattern of conflicting responses to Jesus in John 11. Jesus said that he was "the resurrection and the life" (verse 25) and proved it by raising his friend Lazarus from the dead (verses 43–44). As a result, the people were divided: "Many of the Jews therefore, who had . . . seen what he did, believed in him," but, shockingly, from then on the leaders "made plans to put him to death" (verse 53). Here are two very different responses: placing faith in Jesus or wanting to murder him!

Jesus's Most Significant Week

The most significant week in Jesus's earthly ministry started with what is called his triumphal entry into Jerusalem. Given the pattern mentioned above, we are not surprised that this week also saw conflicting responses to Jesus. Shortly before this event Jesus had raised Lazarus, and many of the people who followed Jesus had witnessed this miracle (John 12:17–18). Others also followed Jesus, so a large crowd was present.

The story of the triumphal entry begins with Jesus's sending two of his disciples to a village nearby. He told them that they would find a donkey, and a colt with her. He instructed the disciples to untie and bring them to him; if anyone asked what they were doing, they were to reply, "The Lord needs them." The disciples found the donkey and colt as Jesus had said and brought them to Jesus. Matthew points out that this is the fulfillment of Old Testament prophecy about the Messiah: "Say to the daughter of Zion, 'Behold, your king is coming to you, humble, and mounted on a donkey, and on a colt, the foal of a beast of burden'" (Matthew 21:5; see also John 12:14–15). Matthew quotes two Old Testament prophecies. The main content of the quotation comes from

Zechariah 9:9, while the phrase "daughter of Zion" is from Isaiah 62:11.

The disciples placed their outer garments on the animals, and Jesus rode the colt into Jerusalem. The people following Jesus laid their garments on the path. Some of the crowd cut palm branches and put these on the path in front of Jesus. Many people poured out of the Eastern Gate of Jerusalem to meet Jesus. As all the people came together, the enthusiasm of the event grew and people started shouting, "Hosanna to the son of David! Blessed is he who comes in the name of the Lord! Hosanna in the highest!"

"Hosanna" is an expression of exaltation and honor. The reference to the "son of David" indicates the crowd was acknowledging Jesus as the descendant of David and the Messiah prophesied in the Old Testament. Those who witnessed the miracle of Jesus raising Lazarus from the dead continually told others in the crowd about it (John 12:17), increasing the excitement. The Pharisees hated all the praise Jesus was getting and appealed to him to stop it: "Teacher, rebuke your disciples." Jesus answered, "I tell you, if these were silent, the very stones would cry out" (Luke 19:39–40).

Jesus Cried over and Prophesied about Jerusalem

As Jesus entered the city, he knew that much of the praise he was receiving was shallow and based on the people's expectation of a political Messiah. The people wanted a political Messiah who would drive out the Romans, who ruled over the Jews. Jesus knew that at the end of the week many of these same people would be calling for him to be crucified. Jesus prophesied about the future of Jerusalem and wept over the people's rejection of him and what he knew was going to happen to the city:

> And when he drew near and saw the city, he wept over it and said, "Would that you, even you, had known on this day the things that make for peace! But now they are hidden from your eyes. For the days will come upon you, when your enemies will set up a barricade around you and surround you and hem you in on every side and tear you down to the ground, you and your children within you. And they will not leave one stone upon another in you, because you did not know the time of your visitation." (Luke 19:42–44)

This prophecy of Jesus was fulfilled in A.D. 70. Titus, the future emperor of Rome, along with Tiberius Julius Alexander, his second-in-command, besieged the city and destroyed it. They killed a large percentage of its inhabitants and completely destroyed the temple.

Jesus's triumphal entry began the last week of his earthly ministry. That Thursday was his Last Supper with his disciples; he was crucified on Friday and rose from the dead the following Sunday. Jesus's triumphal entry is celebrated today in Christian churches on the Sunday before

Easter. It is called Palm Sunday because the crowd cut palm branches and put them on the path before Jesus.

Different Responses to Jesus

Jesus received two radically different responses in the space of a week! Many celebrated his triumphal entry into Jerusalem and proclaimed him to be the long-awaited Messiah and Deliverer. Days later, many—including some who had welcomed him enthusiastically—cried out for his blood. They cried out "Crucify him!" wanting him to endure the shame, torture, and ugly death of one of the most gruesome methods of execution ever devised.

Jesus still receives different responses today. Many give him a warm welcome by trusting him as King of their lives and Savior from sin. Others strongly reject him and want nothing to do with him or people who love him. Many more are indifferent toward him. Perhaps they acknowledge him as a great teacher or example. But they do not want him to interfere with their lives, and they give little thought to him or his claims.

Sometimes a person has two very different responses to Jesus over the course of his life. So it was with Merle. Raised in a rural town in Maine without a church, Merle grew up knowing no one who went to church, and he never gave God much thought. In high school he denied the existence of God and met no opposition. College only reinforced his atheism. No Christians there spoke to him about God or Christianity.

Merle married Donna, his Roman Catholic sweetheart. Once they went camping in Sequoia National Park and met people "mumbling" inside their tent. Later he learned they were praying that God would bring an unsaved person to them. They showed genuine interest in Merle and Donna, who learned that they were all from San Diego. Back home the couple phoned Merle and Donna to try to witness to them. Merle refused to let them mention God, Jesus, church, Sunday school, or their pastor. But they kept showing up with flowers, candy, or gifts for Donna, so he had to let them visit.

One evening, out of frustration on how to approach them with the gospel, the man asked, "Merle, how would you like to learn something about the Bible?" Merle opened his mouth to say "no," but "yes" came out! The man opened a Bible and asked Merle to read Genesis 1:1. He replied, "What is Genesis 1:1?" The man patiently explained it. When Merle read "In the beginning God," he knew there must be a God, and he began to believe. They went from there to Adam and Eve, sin, and what separation from God means in this life and the next. The man explained God's redemptive plan, Jesus Christ, his life, death, and resurrection. That evening Merle argued with and questioned the man for almost seven hours. Merle asked Christ for forgiveness of his sins and to be his Lord and Savior that night, and Donna prayed to receive Christ the next morning.

This happened on a Tuesday, and Wednesday they were in church as two new souls who had been added to the kingdom. A few months later they moved back to his small town in Maine. When they started visiting churches in other towns and meeting people who had known him, some were joyful, while others refused to accept him as a Christian. They did not believe that a sinner such as he could enter the kingdom of God. Years later he went to seminary, and he and Donna served the Lord for many years. Today he heads up a teaching ministry to Ukraine. He gives all the glory to God, who works all things according to his will.

11

Jesus's Last Supper

What do the Jewish Passover and the Lord's Supper have in common? At least three things. First, they are meals in which people enjoy fellowship with one other. Second, they each have to do with death. The Passover commemorates the death of the lambs, which became the main course of the meal after the lambs' blood was put on the house doors. The Lord's Supper commemorates the death of Jesus. Third, they each commemorate a big event. The Passover meal is a reminder of God's deliverance of his people from slavery in Egypt. The Lord's Supper is a reminder that Jesus gave his body and shed his blood to deliver all who trust him to have died in their place.

Jesus Eats the Passover with His Disciples

On the evening before Jesus was crucified, he ate the traditional Passover meal with his disciples. The Passover meal celebrates God's deliverance of the people of Israel from four hundred and thirty years of slavery in Egypt. This deliverance was associated with the last of the ten plagues God brought on Egypt. If you've ever seen the classic movie *The Ten Commandments*, you may remember that God told all the Israelites to kill a lamb and put the blood of the lamb on the doorposts of their houses. Family members were to gather in their houses and eat a meal of the lamb. God said that he would pass over every house that had the blood on its doorposts. However, God would not pass over the Egyptian homes but would kill every firstborn son of the Egyptians in their homes and their firstborn animals. This last plague caused Pharaoh to let the people of Israel go free.

God told the Israelites that every year at that time they were to remember and celebrate this event with the Passover meal. This was the same meal Jesus ate with his disciples just before he went to the cross. Matthew's Gospel says,

> Now on the first day of Unleavened Bread the disciples came to Jesus, saying, "Where will you have us prepare for you to eat the Passover?" He said, "Go into the city to a certain man and say to him, 'The Teacher says, My time is at hand. I will keep

the Passover at your house with my disciples.'"
And the disciples did as Jesus had directed them,
and they prepared the Passover. (Matthew 26:17–
19)

That evening Jesus and his twelve disciples reclined at
the table and ate the Passover meal together. As they
were eating, Jesus told them that one of them was going
to betray him. Each of the disciples asked him, "Is it I?"
He told them that the one who would dip his hand in
the dish with him would betray him, and then he warned,
"The Son of Man goes as it is written of him, but woe to
that man by whom the Son of Man is betrayed! It would
have been better for that man if he had not been born"
(verse 24). Judas, the disciple who was about to betray
Jesus, asked him, "Is it I, Rabbi?" Jesus said that it was
(verse 25).

After this reply, John tells us that "Satan entered into
Judas," and Jesus said to Judas, "What you are going to
do, do quickly" (John 13:27). Judas immediately left
their gathering and went to arrange the betrayal of Jesus.
Judas's betrayal of Jesus was not a surprise to him. He
always knew who it was who would betray him: "Jesus
knew from the beginning who those were who did not
believe, and who it was who would betray him. . . . 'Did
I not choose you, the Twelve? And yet one of you is a
devil.' He spoke of Judas the son of Simon Iscariot, for
he, one of the Twelve, was going to betray him" (6:64,
70–71).

Jesus pointed his disciples to a prophecy from the Psalms: "I am not speaking of all of you; I know whom I have chosen. But the Scripture will be fulfilled, 'He who ate my bread has lifted his heel against me.' I am telling you this now, before it takes place, that when it does take place you may believe that I am he" (John 13:18–19, quoting Psalm 41:9). "Lifting up the heel" means trying to harm someone, perhaps by kicking. So Judas's evil betrayal of Jesus fulfilled a prediction by David in the Psalms and a prediction of Jesus.

Jesus Sets Up the Lord's Supper

As they were eating, Jesus took the bread of the Passover meal and, after blessing it, broke it and gave it to his disciples. He said, "This is my body, which is given for you. Do this in remembrance of me." In the same way, after they had eaten, he took the cup and told them, "This cup that is poured out for you is the new covenant in my blood" (Luke 22:14–20; 1 Corinthians 11:23–26). In saying this, Jesus was pointing to his upcoming death on the cross. He was going to give himself as a substitute offering for sin. His body was going to be broken and his blood spilled so that sinners could be forgiven. He was going to take the death that sin deserves. This is in keeping with Romans 6:23: "The wages of sin is death, but the free gift of God is eternal life in Christ Jesus our Lord."

Just as death passed over the people of Israel's households in the last plague on Egypt because of the lambs' shed blood on their doorposts, Jesus said that eternal death would pass over those believing in him because of his death on the cross: "Truly, truly, I say to you, whoever hears my word and believes him who sent me has eternal life. He does not come into judgment, but has passed from death to life" (John 5:24). It is no wonder, then, that the apostle Paul proclaims, "Christ, our Passover lamb, has been sacrificed" (1 Corinthians 5:7). When Christians today celebrate the Lord's Supper, they remember that they are forgiven of their sins and have a relationship with God through the death and resurrection of Jesus.

After the Passover meal, Jesus informed his disciples, "You will all fall away because of me this night. For it is written, 'I will strike the shepherd, and the sheep of the flock will be scattered'" (Matthew 26:31). Jesus here cites the Old Testament prophet Zechariah (13:7). Peter objected and said, "Though they all fall away because of you, I will never fall away." But Jesus answered him, "Truly, I tell you, this very night, before the rooster crows, you will deny me three times" (Matthew 26:33–34). Peter and the other disciples insisted they would never deny Jesus, but Jesus's prophetic word to Peter and the other disciples was fulfilled that night exactly as he had predicted, as we will see in the next chapter.

Jesus Delivers Us from Death

When the Israelites obeyed God, he passed over their homes and spared them from death.

Death in the Bible means not the end of existence but separation. This is true at three levels. First, physical death is the separation of the soul or spirit from the body. When Jesus died, he called out with a loud voice, "'Father, into your hands I commit my spirit!' And having said this he breathed his last" (Luke 23:46). Jesus's body remained on the cross, but his spirit went immediately into God's presence in heaven. Death for believers means to "be away from the body and at home with the Lord" (2 Corinthians 5:8).

Second, spiritual death means separation from God. Paul speaks of unsaved people as "dead in [their] trespasses and sins" (Ephesians 2:1). Everyone who does not know Christ is spiritually dead, even while being physically alive. They lack the eternal life that comes from God.

Third, the second death means eternal separation from God in hell. John explains, "This is the second death, the lake of fire" (Revelation 20:14), where all unsaved persons go (verse 15). God's passing over the Israelites meant being spared from physical death. All who put their faith in Jesus will be spared from eternal death in the lake of fire.

12

Jesus's Prayer in Gethsemane

Jesus was a man of prayer. He showed this by his example. Luke tells us of Jesus's habit: "He would withdraw to desolate places and pray" (Luke 5:16). What did Jesus do before he chose his twelve disciples? He prayed all night: "In these days he went out to the mountain to pray, and all night he continued in prayer to God" (6:12). After a busy day healing people and casting out demons, Jesus, "rising very early in the morning, while it was still dark . . . departed and went out to a desolate place, and there he prayed" (Mark 1:35). After multiplying loaves of bread and fish to feed over five thousand people, he dismissed the crowds and "went up on the mountain by himself to pray" (Matthew 14:23).

Jesus also proved that he was a man of prayer in his zeal that the temple be put to its proper use. He drove out those who exchanged coins and sold animals, including pigeons, sheep, and oxen (John 2:15), in the temple. The money-changers charged worshipers to exchange their coins for special coins used to pay the temple tax. The animals for sale to worshipers were without blemish and thus guaranteed suitable for sacrifice. But in both cases—coins and animals—the sellers charged high prices. After Jesus drove out the coin exchangers and sellers of animals, he exclaimed, "It is written, 'My house shall be called a house of prayer,' but you make it a den of robbers" (Matthew 21:13).

Some of Jesus's most important prayers were made in anguish. He said, "My soul is very sorrowful, even to death" (Matthew 26:38), and then prayed to the Father three times. And, strange as it sounds, the Father answered these prayers by telling Jesus no.

Jesus Again Predicts His Death and Resurrection

After the Passover meal, Jesus and his eleven disciples (Judas had gone to betray him) sang a hymn and went out to the Mount of Olives. As a prophet, Jesus told them they would all fall away because of him that very night: "For it is written, 'I will strike the shepherd, and the sheep of the flock will be scattered'" (Matthew 26:31; quoting Zechariah 13:7). Jesus also prophesied his resurrection and said, "After I am raised up, I will go before you to Galilee" (Matthew 26:32). This is a dramatic prophecy that assumes, of course, that Jesus was going to die. Three times previously Jesus had told his disciples that he would be killed when he went to Jerusalem but would be resurrected on the third day. Jesus reminded them of these predictions shortly before his arrest and crucifixion.

Peter's Protest and Jesus's Response

When Peter heard Jesus say they would all fall away, he objected: "Though they all fall away because of you, I will never fall away" (Matthew 26:33). Jesus prophesied again and told Peter that before the rooster crowed the next day, he would deny him three times (verse 34). Peter continued to insist he would never deny him, and the other disciples said the same (verse 35). However, just as Jesus said, before the night was out Peter had denied Jesus three times and the other disciples had run away when Jesus was arrested. Why did they not totally abandon Jesus? The answer lies in Jesus's prayer for Peter (and the others) at the time he predicted their falling away: "But I have prayed for you that your faith may not fail. And when you have turned again, strengthen your brothers" (Luke 22:32). Jesus predicted Peter and the other disciples' failure. He also predicted that they would return to Jesus and serve him. His love and prayer for them would keep them from falling totally away from him and would ensure their return.

Jesus's Agonizing Prayer in the Garden of Gethsemane

Jesus and the disciples then went to the Garden of Gethsemane, located on the western slope of the Mount of Olives. Jesus told most of his disciples to wait for him while he went a little farther to pray. He took Peter, James, and John with him and told them, "Watch with me." He then went a little farther, fell on his face, and prayed, "My Father, if it be possible, let this cup pass from me; nevertheless, not as I will, but as you will" (Matthew 26:39). After praying this, Jesus went back to Peter, James, and John and found them sleeping. He asked them, "So, could you not watch with me one hour? Watch and pray that you may not enter into temptation. The spirit indeed is willing, but the flesh is weak" (Matthew 26:40–41).

Jesus knew the disciples were about to be tempted to desert him, and he urged them to pray so that they wouldn't fail at that temptation. Jesus left them and prayed again, "My Father, if this cannot pass unless I drink it, your will be done." He returned and found the three disciples sleeping again. He left them once more and prayed the same thing. An angel appeared to him and strengthened him. "And being in agony he prayed more earnestly; and his sweat became like great drops of blood falling down to the ground" (Luke 22:43–44).

In agony three times Jesus asked his Father to remove the cross from him, and three times the Father said no to his beloved Son's prayer. Jesus did not sin when he prayed in this way, because, as much as he wanted to be delivered from the terrible death on the cross, each time he submitted to the Father's will. Why did Jesus undergo such agonizing prayer? It was for us sinners and our salvation.

Jesus Will Suffer Physical and Spiritual Death

Jesus knew that his impending death on the cross was not just an agonizing physical death but would involve separation from his Father's love and fellowship. On the cross Jesus cried out, "My God, my God, why have you forsaken me?" (Matthew 27:46). The eternal fellowship and love between the Father and Son was interrupted. We cannot fully understand this terrible separation. It did not mean a breaking apart of the Trinity, but it did affect the relationship between the Father and the Son. Their fellowship was disturbed when Jesus bore the guilt of and judgment against sinners in their place. Jesus returned again to his disciples in the garden and told them, "See, the hour is at hand, and the Son of Man is betrayed into the hands of sinners. Rise, let us be going; see, my betrayer is at hand" (Matthew 26:45–46).

Thankfully, after Jesus made atonement for sin on the cross, his relationship with the Father was repaired. For, as he died, "Jesus, calling out with a loud voice, said, 'Father, into your hands I commit my spirit!' And having said this he breathed his last" (Luke 23:46).

What Do Jesus's Prayers Have to Do with Us?

Jesus's agonizing prayers in Gethsemane have much to do with us. He went to the cross knowing full well what it would mean: bearing "our sins in his body on the tree" (1 Peter 2:24) and temporary separation from his Father's love (Matthew 27:46). We could never pay for our own sins. The psalmist declares, "Truly no man can ransom another, or give to God the price of his life" (Psalm 49:7). Thankfully, Jesus did for us what we could not do. He said of himself, "The Son of Man came not to be served but to serve, and to give his life as a ransom for many" (Matthew 20:28).

So, even while we are shocked at the Father's saying no to the prayers of Jesus, his Son, we should be thankful. Our hearts should be grateful that Jesus loved us so much that he give his life as a ransom for us when he died in our place. What can we do but trust him for loving us like this? "Lord Jesus, we thank you for dying on the cross for sinners like us. We put all our confidence for salvation in your death in our place. We rejoice in your resurrection, and give our lives to you to be used for your glory. Amen."

13

Jesus's Betrayal, Arrest, and Denial

J esus lived on earth for thirty-three and a half years, the last week of which was tumultuous. One of his disciples betrayed him to death, and Jesus was arrested. Another, who professed a willingness to die for Jesus, denied him three times when Jesus was arrested. Through it all, however, Jesus remained faithful and allowed nothing to deter him from his mission of dying on the cross for rebels like us. Judas and Peter stand as examples of turning away from God and of different responses to falling.

Jesus's Betrayal

After Judas left the Passover meal with Jesus and the other disciples, he went to the high priests and other religious leaders to betray Jesus. These authorities were ready for any word from Judas concerning an ideal place to arrest Jesus apart from the crowds. Before the Passover meal they had made a deal with Judas concerning where they could capture Jesus. The devil prompted Judas:

> Then Satan entered into Judas called Iscariot, who was of the number of the twelve. He went away and conferred with the chief priests and officers how he might betray him to them. And they were glad, and agreed to give him money. So he consented and sought an opportunity to betray him to them in the absence of a crowd. (Luke 22:3–6)

For his efforts Judas was paid thirty pieces of silver (Matthew 26:15). This fulfilled a prediction in Zechariah 11:12 that the Messiah would be betrayed for thirty pieces of silver. This is another remarkable fulfillment of prophecy. Zechariah predicted the exact amount of silver that would be paid and predicted that later it would be thrown on the floor of the temple and used to buy a potter's field, a place to bury destitute people. That is exactly what happened. After he betrayed Jesus, Judas regretted his actions and threw the silver on the floor of the temple. The Jewish religious leaders didn't want it back, so they used it to buy a potter's field.

Jesus's Arrest

When Judas went to the Jewish leaders, they were ready for action. They had their posse ready to go at a word from Judas. He led them to the Garden of Gethsemane, where he knew Jesus often went in the evening. While Jesus was speaking with his disciples and urging them to pray so they would not enter into temptation, Judas arrived with a large crowd, consisting of the chief priests and the elders of the people, along with temple guards, soldiers, and servants. They were carrying swords and clubs (Matthew 26:47; Luke 22:47, 52). Judas had given them a sign that the one he greeted with a kiss would be Jesus. Judas approached Jesus to kiss him and identify him, but Jesus asked, "Judas, would you betray the Son of Man with a kiss?"

The disciples around Jesus saw what was happening and asked, "Lord, shall we strike with the sword?" (Luke 22:48–49). Peter drew his sword and struck Malchus, the servant of the high priest, and cut off his right ear. Jesus said "No more of this!" and touched his ear and healed him (22:50–51; John 18:10–11). Jesus commanded the disciples to put away their swords: "Put your sword back into its place. For all who take the sword will perish by the sword. Do you think that I cannot appeal to my Father, and he will at once send me more than twelve legions of angels? But how then should the Scriptures be fulfilled, that it must be so?" (Matthew 26:52–54).

At this word all the disciples fled, which fulfilled another prophecy. At the Last Supper Jesus had told his disciples that they would all be scattered in keeping with the words of Zechariah 13:7: "Strike the shepherd, and the sheep will be scattered." Once again an Old Testament prediction of events in Jesus's life was fulfilled. The posse seized Jesus and brought him to the house of Caiaphas, the high priest.

Jesus's Denials by Peter

As mentioned, after Jesus's arrest the posse took him to the house of Caiaphas, the high priest. Annas, Caiaphas's father-in-law, also occupied this house (Matthew 26:57–58; John 18:13, 15, 24). These houses often had a courtyard that looked into the interior of the house. Peter and another disciple, presumably John, followed at a distance. A fire was burning in the middle of the courtyard, and some of the guards were sitting around it. John knew someone at the gate and obtained entrance for Peter, who joined the people at the fire and sat down by it. Most of the soldiers had probably already returned to the Fortress of Antonia after delivering their prisoner. While Jesus's trials were going on, Peter denied Jesus, just as Jesus had prophesied a few hours before.

A servant girl came up to Peter, obviously suspicious of him. The fact that John (the other disciple) had secured Peter's entrance into the courtyard might have aroused her suspicions. She looked at Peter and pro-claimed, "This man was also with Jesus." Earlier, Peter had loudly announced his unswerving loyalty for Jesus, but now a servant girl's accusation scared him, and he denied Jesus. He answered her, "Woman, I do not know him" (Luke 22:56–57). Peter's second denial of Jesus came just a little later. Someone else said to him, "You are also one of them." Peter answered, "Man, I am not" (verse 58). Matthew adds that Peter uttered an oath with this denial (Matthew 26:72). About an hour later another man began to insist that Peter was with Jesus because Peter was a Galilean (Peter's accent identified him as such): "After a little while the bystanders came up and said to Peter, 'Certainly you too are one of them, for your accent betrays you.'" Peter invoked a curse on himself and swore, "I do not know the man!" (26:73).

About this time, Jesus's night trial had ended, and he was being led across the courtyard. While Peter was still speaking, a rooster crowed and Jesus turned and looked at Peter, who was instantly reminded of the prophetic word Jesus had spoken to him just a few hours earlier: "Before the rooster crows today, you will deny me three times" (Luke 22:34). Peter saw Jesus looking at him and heard the rooster crowing, and the words of Jesus echoed in his mind. He ran out and wept bitterly. His heart was filled with genuine regret and sorrow for his weakness and denial of Jesus. He not only fulfilled Jesus's prophecy that he would betray him but also demonstrated the truth of Jeremiah 17:9: "The heart is deceitful about all things and desperately sick; who can understand it?"

Judas and Peter

Scripture vividly contrasts the stories of Judas and Peter. Judas, the disciple who betrayed Jesus, committed suicide. Admitting that he had sinned (Matthew 27:4), he committed suicide by hanging. Peter provides more detail when he says that, presumably after hanging himself, Judas fell headlong and "burst open in the middle and all his bowels gushed out" (Acts 1:18).

Like Judas, Peter sinned against Jesus, denying him three times. Unlike Judas, Peter repented of his sin, and, after the resurrection, Jesus restored Peter and showed the abundant mercy of God and the forgiveness available to those who believe in Jesus (John 21:15–17).

Today, some resemble Judas and some Peter. Those who profess Christ but deny him by the way they live should pay attention to Judas's life and end. He was Jesus's disciple, heard his messages, and saw his miracles. Even when he came to betray Jesus, Jesus called him a "friend" (Matthew 26:50). May God help us not to be false believers like Judas (Acts 1:25)!

Peter was far from perfect. After boasting that he would never fall away from Jesus (Matthew 26:33), he denied Jesus three times! The Bible does not present any sinless people (except Jesus!). "All have sinned and fall short of the glory of God" (Romans 3:23). But the good news is that God loves sinners and gave his Son to die for all who believe in him. That includes Peter, who showed the genuineness of his faith by turning from his sin and reaffirming his love for and faith in Jesus. May God give us grace to be like Peter!

14

Jesus's Trials, Part 1

J esus's trials are similar to ours in some ways and very different in others. Before we look at the trials that led to Jesus's death on the cross, an overview of the events would be helpful. Jesus endured two types of trials. Part of his trials were before the Sanhedrin, the Jewish religious council, and others were civil trials before Pontius Pilate, the Roman governor, and Herod, the Roman king of Judea. Each of these trials had three stages. The three stages of the religious trial were (1) a preliminary hearing before Annas (John 18:12–14, 19–23); (2) the trial before the Sanhedrin at night (Matthew 26:57–68; Mark 14:55–65); and (3) the trial before the same body early in the morning (Matthew 27:1–2; Mark 15:1; Luke 22:66–71). The three stages of the civil trial were (1) the first trial before Pilate; (2) the trial before Herod; (3) the final trial before Pilate.

Even though Jesus's appearances before the Jewish bodies are presented as trials, these leaders had already decided to put him to death (John 11:49–50). The truth is that these trials were really a farce.

Jesus's Preliminary Hearing before Annas

Annas had been the high priest in Judea from A.D. 6 to 15. Procurator Gratus deposed him when Annas was 36 years old. However, Annas still held great influence and power in Israel. His son-in-law was Caiaphas, the official high priest, and Annas exercised power through him. Jesus was first brought to Annas for examination. John 18:13–14 states, "First they led him to Annas, for he was the father-in-law of Caiaphas, who was high priest that year. It was Caiaphas who had advised the Jews that it would be expedient that one man should die for the people." They questioned Jesus about his teaching. He told them that he had spoken openly in the synagogue and temple and said nothing in secret. Jesus admitted that information about his teaching was available from people who had heard it. Essentially, Jesus refused to testify against himself. When Jesus said this, one of the guards slapped him in the face and rebuked him for speaking this way to the authorities. But "Jesus answered him, 'If what I said is wrong, bear witness about the wrong; but if what I said is right, why do you strike me?'" (John 18:23). This guard had not even been ordered to hit Jesus. Annas then sent Jesus to Caiaphas. The preliminary hearing had given Caiaphas time to gather some of the members of the Sanhedrin.

Peter had been following at a distance and managed to get into the high priest's outer courtyard. He was warming himself by a fire when someone came to him and questioned him. This led to a dramatic event in the life of Peter: his denial of Jesus.

Jesus's Trial before the Sanhedrin at Night

After Peter's denial of Jesus, as he had predicted, our story returns to Jesus's trial. That night Jesus was brought before part of the Sanhedrin, the Jewish ruling council. Not all of the members were present. They attempted to find witnesses to testify against Jesus so that they could put him to death. The reason for this mock trial was so they could go to Pilate and demand that Jesus be put to death. They questioned many false witnesses, whose testimonies did not agree (Matthew 26:59–60; Mark 14:55–56).

Finally, two false witnesses came forward and testified that Jesus had boasted, "I am able to destroy the temple of God, and to rebuild it in three days" (Matthew 26:61–62). This is a misquote of what Jesus had said in John 2:19: "Destroy this temple, and in three days I will raise it up." Jesus was referring to himself and the future resurrection of his body after three days. He did not say that he himself would destroy the temple. They were testifying that Jesus was a defamer of the temple. Jesus could

have defended himself and explained how this was a misquote and a misinterpretation of what he had said, but he
remained silent. "And the high priest stood up and said,
'Have you no answer to make? What is it that these men
testify against you?' But Jesus remained silent" (Matthew
26:62–63). Here once more Jesus fulfilled Old Testament prophecy concerning the Messiah: "He was oppressed, and he was afflicted, yet he opened not his
mouth; like a lamb that is led to the slaughter, and like a
sheep that before its shearers is silent, so he opened not
his mouth" (Isaiah 53:7). Isaiah spoke these words when
describing the Servant of the Lord, who would die in
place of his people: "He was crushed for our iniquities"
(verse 6).

Then the trial took a dramatic turn. Caiaphas stood
up and asked Jesus a decisive question directly and under
oath before God: "I adjure you by the living God, tell us
if you are the Christ, the Son of God" (Matthew 26:63).
The high priest demanded that Jesus answer "by the living God," which is asking him to answer under a solemn
oath. "And Jesus said, 'I am, and you will see the Son of
Man seated at the right hand of Power, and coming with
the clouds of heaven'" (Mark 14:62). Jesus made a self-
identification based on Daniel 7:13–14, an Old Testament prophetic passage referring to the Messiah. The
high priest immediately recognized this passage and what
Jesus's self-identification meant. Jesus said that he was
the fulfillment of Daniel's prophecy: he is the one who

would come with the clouds of heaven, would have authority to judge the nations, and would have an eternal kingdom. When Jesus applied this prophecy to himself, he identified himself as the Messiah and as God.

The high priest and the other members of the Sanhedrin were outraged at Jesus's self-identification: "Then the high priest tore his robes and said, 'He has uttered blasphemy. What further witnesses do we need? You have now heard his blasphemy. What is your judgment?' They answered, 'He deserves death'" (Matthew 26:65–66).

The men keeping Jesus in custody began to mock him. They spit in his face, beat him, and slapped him. They blindfolded him and taunted him, saying, "Prophesy to us, you Christ! Who is it that struck you?" (Matthew 26:67–68).

Jesus's Trial before the Sanhedrin Early in the Morning

After this the Bible briefly mentions a short morning meeting of the Sanhedrin: "When morning came, all the chief priests and the elders of the people took counsel against Jesus to put him to death" (Matthew 27:1). This was an attempt to present a picture of legality regarding their trial of Jesus at night. They had already condemned Jesus as worthy of death. However, they did not have the right under Roman rule to execute anyone. Therefore they took him to Pontius Pilate, the Roman governor, as we will see in the next chapter.

Jesus's Trials and Ours

The trials Jesus endured are similar to ours in some ways and very different in others. Whether or not we are ever on trial in a court of law, we all undergo trials and tests of life. The Bible tells us that Jesus did the same: "We do not have a high priest who is unable to sympathize with our weaknesses, but one who in every respect has been tempted as we are, yet without sin" (Hebrews 4:15). However, the last three words in this verse—"yet without sin"—set Jesus apart from all of us. None of us is without sin. In fact, we all sin in thoughts and words, and sometimes in actions, too. But although Jesus was tempted and tried in ways we never will be, he never sinned.

This underscores another difference between Jesus's trials and ours. His fulfilled Old Testament predictions made centuries before. He fulfilled prophecy because of his identity: he was the promised Son of God and Deliverer of all who trust him. So, here again, examining Jesus's life in terms of prophecy puts the spotlight on him as the only Savior of the world. All who bow the knee before him and trust him as Lord know that he is with them in their trials. And that is very good news indeed!

15

Jesus's Trials, Part 2

Injustice is terrible. Christians find solace in the fact
that in the end God will make things right. In the
meantime, many wrongs go unpunished. This is the case
with horrible wrongs done to God's sinless Son in the
trials he endured, leading to his death by the torture of
crucifixion.

In the last chapter we looked at Jesus's trials before
the Jews. These included his preliminary hearing before
Annas, the retired high priest, and his trials before the
Sanhedrin, the Jewish religious council, at night and in
the morning. Here we look at Jesus's three trials before
Gentiles: Pontius Pilate, the Roman governor; Herod,
the Roman king of Judea; and Pilate again. All of these
trials speak of the injustice of sinful human beings con-
demning the spotless Son of God to death for crimes he
did not commit.

Jesus's First Trial before Pontius Pilate

Pilate asked the Jewish leaders to provide more detailed information concerning the charges they were leveling against Jesus: "'What accusation do you bring against this man?' They answered him, 'If this man were not doing evil, we would not have delivered him over to you'" (John 18:29–30). Upon receiving this ambiguous answer, Pilate told them to judge Jesus according to their own law. The Jewish leaders told Pilate that they did not have the authority to execute anyone. They had already condemned Jesus to death in the night meeting of the Sanhedrin and obviously wanted Jesus to be killed. The type of death the Romans would inflict upon Jesus as a Jew would be crucifixion. Those who were not Roman citizens and were found guilty of treason against Rome would usually be crucified. John's Gospel points out that this was a fulfillment of Jesus's prophecy concerning the death he would undergo: "This was to fulfill the word that Jesus had spoken to show by what kind of death he was going to die" (John 18:32).

Pilate had Jesus brought into the governor's residence and began to question him. Pilate asked Jesus, "Are you the king of the Jews?" Jesus asked Pilate if he was asking this of his own accord or merely because he had heard the Jewish leaders say it. Pilate noted that it was Jesus's own nation and chief priests who handed him over to him, and he asked him what he had done. Jesus then made an important statement about his kingship: "My kingdom is not of this world. If my kingdom were of this world, my servants would have been fighting, that I might not be delivered over to the Jews. But my kingdom is not from the world" (John 18:36). Pilate replied, "So you are a king?" Jesus replied, "You say that I am a king. For this purpose I was born and for this purpose I have come into the world—to bear witness to the truth. Everyone who is of the truth listens to my voice" (John 18:37). Jesus again said that he was a king but, as he explained, not an earthly king. Pilate was curious: how could a man claim to be a king but not rule over an earthly nation? Jesus implied his incarnation in the statement that he came into this world. He came from heaven's glory to "save his people from their sins" (Matthew 1:21).

Pilate responded to Jesus's statement that he came to bear witness to the truth by asking, "What is truth?" Pilate then returned to his outer porch and told the Jewish leaders that he didn't find any guilt in Jesus. The Jews continued to accuse Jesus of troublemaking and mentioned that "He stirs up people throughout all Judea, from Galilee to this place" (Luke 23:5). When Pilate heard that Jesus was from Galilee, he said he belonged to Herod's jurisdiction and sent him to Herod. Roman law allowed a man to be tried in the province where the crime was allegedly committed. Jesus's accusers might have thought the point that Jesus was from Galilee would help persuade Pilate to put him to death. Numerous conflicts had arisen in Galilee involving Zealots, Jews wanting to rebel violently against Rome, and those practicing guerrilla warfare tactics against Rome. They reasoned that if they could link Jesus with that region, it might help their case against him before Pilate. However, Pilate attempted to get rid of the case.

Jesus's Appearance before Herod

Multiple kings are named Herod in the New Testament. The Herod to whom Jesus was sent was Herod Antipas, son of Herod the Great, who had the male babies killed in Bethlehem in an attempt to kill Jesus. John the Baptist had rebuked Herod Antipas for committing adultery with his brother's wife, and Herod had put John in prison and had him beheaded (Matthew 14:1–12). When Herod heard about Jesus's miracles, he wondered if John the Baptist had been raised from the dead: "At that time Herod the tetrarch heard about the fame of Jesus, and he said to his servants, 'This is John the Baptist. He has been raised from the dead; that is why these miraculous powers are at work in him'" (Matthew 14:1–2). Herod was glad to see Jesus and was hoping to see him perform some sign. He wanted Jesus to entertain him. He questioned Jesus, but Jesus did not answer him. While Herod was doing so, the chief priests and the scribes were continuing their accusations against Jesus (Luke 23:9–10). Herod's response to Jesus's silence was to mock and ridicule him. His soldiers treated Jesus harshly, put a beautiful kingly robe on him, and sent him back to Pilate. Luke notes that Herod and Pilate had been enemies but from that day forward became friends.

Jesus's Second Trial before Pontius Pilate

Pilate called together the chief priests, the rulers, and the people and told them that neither he nor Herod found anything in Jesus to substantiate the charges against him. Jesus had done nothing that deserved the death penalty, and thus Pilate would simply punish him and release him. However, the people before him were becoming increasingly agitated, and Pilate wanted to get rid of the case and defuse the situation.

A custom during the feast of Passover was for the governor to release one prisoner the people wanted. Pilate asked the people whom they wanted released, Jesus or Barabbas, a notorious prisoner and murderer. The chief priests and elders had persuaded the crowd to ask for Barabbas, and they cried out for him. Pilate asked them what he should do with Jesus. They all yelled, "Let him be crucified!" Pilate asked, "Why, what has he done?" The crowd shouted all the more, "Let him be crucified!"

Pilate had Jesus whipped. The soldiers twisted together a crown of thorns and put it on his head. They put a purple robe on him and came up to him saying, "Hail, King of the Jews!" They mocked and struck him. Pilate told the people again that he found no guilt in Jesus, and then he brought him out before them. Jesus was wearing the crown of thorns and purple robe. Pilate exclaimed, "Behold the man!" Jesus was weak, bloody, and beaten. Perhaps Pilate thought the flogging, mocking, and beating of Jesus would appease the Jewish leaders and the people with them.

However, when the chief priests and officers saw Jesus, they cried out, "Crucify him, crucify him!" Pilate once again told them that he found no guilt in him. The Jews answered, "We have a law, and according to that law he ought to die because he has made himself the Son of God" (John 19:7). This statement concerned Pilate, and he brought Jesus back into his headquarters. He asked Jesus, "Where are you from?" Jesus remained silent. Pilate said, "You will not speak to me? Do you not know that I have authority to release you and authority to crucify you?" Jesus told him, "You would have no authority over me at all unless it had been given you from above. Therefore, he who delivered me over to you has the greater sin" (John 19:10–11). Jesus could have been referring to Judas, who betrayed him, but more likely he was referring to the immediate person in charge of turning him over to Pilate: Caiaphas. Pilate was responsible to God for his sin in his injustice to Jesus, but Caiaphas had the greater sin.

From that moment on Pilate tried to release Jesus. He had believed that Jesus was innocent of treason against

Rome all along, but now he made greater efforts to release Jesus. However, the Jews began to yell, "If you release this man, you are not Caesar's friend. Everyone who makes himself a king opposes Caesar" (John 19:12). They implied that they would lodge a complaint against Pilate with Emperor Tiberias. Pilate saw that a riot was beginning. He took water and washed his hands before the crowd, saying, "I am innocent of this man's blood; see to it yourselves" (Matthew 27:24). They answered, "His blood be on us and on our children!" (verse 25). Pilate released Barabbas and had Jesus scourged. As a prelude to crucifixion, Roman soldiers beat the accused with a whip of leather embedded with pieces of bone or lead. This dreaded beating weakened the victim, sometimes to the point of death. Pilate then delivered him to be crucified.

The Greatest Injustice

Of course, Jesus committed none of the crimes the false witnesses brought forward. What about the high priests' charge of blasphemy? It too was false, for Jesus truly was "the Christ, the Son of God" (Matthew 26:63). Jesus "committed no sin, neither was deceit found in his mouth" (1 Peter 2:22, quoting Isaiah 53:9). Jesus's innocence raises more questions. Why didn't he fight back when falsely accused? And what was his purpose in submitting to such grave injustice and suffering?

Jesus did not fight back because he was determined to do his Father's will: "When he was reviled, he did not revile in return; when he suffered, he did not threaten, but continued entrusting himself to him who judges justly" (1 Peter 2:23). Jesus's greater purpose in all of this was to rescue sinners like us: "He himself bore our sins in his body on the tree" (verse 24). Jesus died in our place. He, the holy One, died in the place of us, the unholy ones.

And the great news is that all who acknowledge their sins and turn to Jesus in faith are healed spiritually by his wounds on the cross: "By his wounds you have been healed" (verse 24). Peter likens us to lost sheep: "You were straying like sheep, but have now returned to the Shepherd and Overseer of your souls" (verse 25). Jesus is the Good Shepherd who loves and redeems all who believe in him for salvation. He is our Lord, our Overseer, who loved us and gave himself for us. Ironically, the greatest injustice brings forgiveness and eternal life to believers in Jesus. Surely we have much to be thankful for.

PART 5

Prophecies of Jesus's Death

16

Jesus's Crucifixion, Part 1

The crucifixion of Jesus fulfilled many Old Testament prophecies. Amazingly, all of these predictions were made at least four hundred years before Jesus's birth—and most of them long before that. They are not vague prophecies open to various interpretations but foretell specific events that took place during Jesus's crucifixion. Isaiah 53 as a whole predicts and explains Jesus's death and its meaning. Psalm 22 also contains important prophecies concerning Jesus's death. Other fulfilled predictions include Psalm 34:20, Psalm 69:20–21, and Zechariah 12:10. We will consider these prophecies as they appear in Jesus's story.

Jesus Goes to the Cross

After Pilate condemned Jesus to be crucified, he had him scourged (Matthew 27:26). This was common for those who were to be crucified. It would weaken the person and hasten death. Scourging was the most terrible of beatings. The victim was stripped and tied to a post; several torturers would beat him until they were exhausted or the commanding officer stopped the beating. The instrument used was a whip with leather thongs fitted with pieces of bone or metal. Sometimes the victim died from the scourging. Eyewitnesses report that a brutal scourging could leave a victim's bones and entrails exposed. This is part of what Jesus endured in his suffering and death to save his people from their sins. As noted earlier, Isaiah's prophecy was being fulfilled: "He was wounded for our transgressions; he was crushed for our iniquities; upon him was the chastisement that brought us peace, and with his stripes we are healed" (Isaiah 53:5). This scourging explains why Jesus was unable to carry his cross.

Customarily, executions took place outside the city, and those who were to be crucified had to carry their own cross. At first Jesus carried his own cross (John 19:17), but he was so weak that he couldn't continue. This is understandable when we consider all that he had endured over the last fifteen hours. At the Last Supper he saw Judas leave to betray him and Peter loudly proclaim he would never deny him. He experienced emotional anguish as he prayed in the Garden of Gethsemane. Then Judas betrayed him, he was arrested, his disciples deserted

him, and he experienced the hypocritical trials before Annas and the Sanhedrin. He was mocked and ridiculed in
the palace of Caiaphas, and he heard his trusted disciple
Peter deny him.

He was taken to Pilate and then sent to Herod, where
he was also mocked. He was taken back to Pilate and
questioned. He heard the same crowd that had shouted
"Hosanna!" just a few days before ask for the criminal
Barabbas to be released instead of him and cry out for
him to be crucified. After Pilate condemned him to be
crucified, he experienced a Roman scourging and more
ridicule from the soldiers. It is amazing he could carry his
cross for any distance at all! When Jesus could not carry
his cross any further, the soldiers requisitioned a man
nearby, Simon from Cyrene, to carry Jesus's cross. Luke
informs us that were was a large crowd of people following Jesus and Simon. Women in the crowd were beating
their breasts and mourning and grieving for Jesus (Luke
23:27). Jesus turned to them and said,

> Daughters of Jerusalem, do not weep for me, but
> weep for yourselves and for your children. For be-
> hold, the days are coming when they will say,
> "Blessed are the barren and the wombs that never
> bore and the breasts that never nursed!" Then
> they will begin to say to the mountains, "Fall on
> us," and to the hills, "Cover us." For if they do
> these things when the wood is green, what will
> happen when it is dry? (Luke 23:28–31)

Jesus knew he was facing incredible agony in the next few hours. He knew he would be suffering the torments of hell on the cross to redeem people from their sins. But he also knew that his future was sure. He had already prophesied to his disciples that he would rise from the dead. However, if there was no repentance in Jerusalem, the future of those people was not secure. In A.D. 70 the Romans destroyed the city and the temple in a military campaign.

Jesus Is Crucified

Jesus, along with two criminals to be crucified with him, came to a place called the Skull. The soldiers offered Jesus a mixture of wine and myrrh to help with pain (Matthew 27:34). Jesus tasted it and then refused it. This fulfilled Scripture: "Reproaches have broken my heart, so that I am in despair. I looked for pity, but there was none, and for comforters, but I found none. They gave me poison for food, and for my thirst they gave me sour wine to drink" (Psalm 69:20–21). There they crucified Jesus along with the criminals, one on his right and one on his left (Matthew 27:38). His crucifixion between two criminals fulfilled more Old Testament prophecies: "They made his grave with the wicked" (Isaiah 53:9), and "He was numbered with the transgressors" (verse 12). In fact, the whole of Isaiah 53 was fulfilled in these events. The Gospels do not go into detail concerning how the nails were driven into Jesus's hands and feet. The Bible places its emphasis on the fact that Jesus was giving himself as an offering for sin while he was on the cross.

Events during the Crucifixion

As Jesus was crucified, he made his first statement from the cross. It was a prayer to his Father: "Father, forgive them, for they know not what they do" (Luke 23:34). The soldiers were simply following orders to crucify someone. They had no idea that Jesus was really God incarnate. Many in Jerusalem were just following the urgings of the Jewish leaders to shout for Jesus to be crucified. Part of the answer to Jesus's prayer could have been the thousands of new Jewish believers as the gospel began to be proclaimed in Jerusalem and Judea (Acts 2:37–47; 4:4). Even many priests came to believe in Jesus (6:7). Jesus's prayer was a fulfillment of Isaiah 53:12: "He bore the sin of many, and makes intercession for the transgressors."

Pontius Pilate wrote an inscription that was nailed on the cross above Jesus. It was a common practice to post a sign like this stating the crime for which a person was being crucified. Pilate wrote in Hebrew, Latin, and Greek "Jesus of Nazareth, the King of the Jews." The chief priests complained to Pilate about what he had written and wanted it changed to read "This man said, 'I am King of the Jews.'" Pilate answered them, "What I have written I have written" (John 19:19–22).

After the Roman soldiers crucified Jesus, they cast lots to divide his garments among themselves (Matthew 27:35). These garments included his headgear, sandals, belt, outer garment, and seamless tunic, woven all the way from top to bottom. They divided the other garments among themselves but did not tear the seamless tunic. This fulfilled Psalm 22:18, as John relates:

> When the soldiers had crucified Jesus, they took his garments and divided them into four parts, one part for each soldier; also his tunic. But the tunic was seamless, woven in one piece from top to bottom, so they said to one another, "Let us not tear it, but cast lots for it to see whose it shall be." This was to fulfill the Scripture which says, "They divided my garments among them, and for my clothing they cast lots." (John 19:23–24)

Psalm 22 is an important prophetic psalm setting forth many of the events of Jesus's crucifixion. It was written approximately one thousand years before Jesus. The fulfilled prophecies of this psalm again demonstrate the supernatural character of the Bible.

The Reaction of Various People to Jesus on the Cross

The Gospels describe the reaction of various groups of people to Jesus: scribes and Jewish rulers, passersby, soldiers, and the men who were crucified with Jesus. Many people were gathered in Jerusalem for the Passover Feast.

Some passed by and observed the scene. Some of those who were passing by ridiculed Jesus and taunted him: "Those who passed by derided him, wagging their heads and saying, 'You who would destroy the temple and rebuild it in three days, save yourself! If you are the Son of God, come down from the cross'" (Matthew 27:39–40). This is a slanderous misinterpretation of what Jesus had said in John 2:19. Remember, at that time he was speaking of his own body and his resurrection on the third day. These people stated that it was weakness and inability that kept Jesus on the cross. Ironically, the opposite was true. Jesus was still God in the flesh, and it was a tremendous restraint of his power and an exercise of his mercy and love for sinners that kept him on the cross. The Old Testament also prophesied this:

> I am a worm and not a man, scorned by mankind and despised by the people. All who see me mock me; they make mouths at me; they wag their heads; "He trusts in the LORD; let him deliver him; let him rescue him, for he delights in him!" (Psalm 22:6–8)

> This is the word that the LORD has spoken concerning him: "She despises you, she scorns you— the virgin daughter of Zion; she wags her head behind you—the daughter of Jerusalem. Whom have you mocked and reviled? Against whom have you raised your voice and lifted your eyes to the

heights? Against the Holy One of Israel!" (Isaiah 37:22–23)

The chief priest, scribes, and the elders were also mocking Jesus. They lost all sense of dignity. Their words were similar to the ones of those passing by and also fulfilled Psalm 22:8.

> So also the chief priests, with the scribes and elders, mocked him, saying, "He saved others; he cannot save himself. He is the King of Israel; let him come down now from the cross, and we will believe in him. He trusts in God; let God deliver him now, if he desires him. For he said, 'I am the Son of God.'" (Matthew 27:41–43)

They ridiculed Jesus's claim that he was the Son of God and said that he should come down from the cross. It is interesting, however, that the ones passing by spoke directly to Jesus. The Jewish leaders spoke only to themselves in mocking Jesus. This reflects their intense hatred for Jesus, the same hatred that led to their plotting his murder and demanding his execution.

The soldiers who crucified him joined in mocking Jesus. Similar to the other people ridiculing him, they said, "If you are the king of the Jews, save yourself" (Luke 23:27). Even one of the men who was crucified with Jesus reviled him, saying, "Are you not the Christ? Save yourself and us!" However, the other criminal rebuked him, asking, "Do you not fear God, since you are under the same sentence of condemnation?" This man then added an important statement, "And we indeed justly, for we are receiving the due reward of our deeds; but this man has done nothing wrong." And he asked, "Jesus, remember me when you come into your kingdom" (Luke 23:39–42).

One of the criminals expressed repentance and faith in Jesus. The man threw himself on Jesus's mercy and asked to be remembered in his kingdom. He expressed faith that, even though Jesus was dying on the cross, he would have a kingdom. In response Jesus promised him, "Truly, I say to you, today you will be with me in paradise" (Luke 23:43). Paradise is simply another word for heaven. Jesus gave him wonderful assurance of his salvation. Many people have received comfort from this event. They have come to saving faith in Jesus near the end of their lives and have seen that salvation is possible even in the last moments of life. It also emphasizes that salvation is a gift of God and not by our works. The man on the cross had no opportunity to do any works to try to earn God's favor; he was saved only by God's grace in Jesus.

Jesus Provides for His Mother

In Jewish culture it was customary for the oldest son to provide for his widowed mother. Even while suffering on the cross, Jesus remembered his mother and made provision for her. John was the only disciple at the foot of the cross. He was with Mary, the mother of Jesus. "When Jesus saw his mother and the disciple whom he loved standing nearby, he said to his mother, 'Woman, behold, your son!' Then he said to the disciple, 'Behold, your mother!' And from that hour the disciple took her to his own home" (John 19:26–27). This demonstrates Jesus's obedience to God's commands. In this action he kept the Fifth Commandment and honored his mother in providing care and security for her. The most dramatic and important aspect of Jesus's crucifixion happened next and is the subject of our next chapter.

17

Jesus's Crucifixion, Part 2

Jesus Makes Atonement for Sins

After Jesus hung on the cross for three hours, an unusual thing happened: the land grew suddenly dark. This darkness lasted for the last three hours that Jesus was on the cross and signified God's judgment on sin. During that time Jesus satisfied the justice of God due to sinners. Jesus suffered the judgment of hell as our substitute. Jesus had said earlier that he had come to "give his life a ransom for many" (Mark 10:45). At the Last Supper he had spoken of his body broken and his blood poured out for the forgiveness of sins (Matthew 26:26–28). Now the event to which those words pointed came to pass. Jesus suffered intense agony and terrible isolation from his Father. He was bearing God's judgment in the place of sinners. This fulfilled Isaiah's prophecy:

He was wounded for our transgressions; he was crushed for our iniquities; upon him was the chastisement that brought us peace, and with his stripes we are healed. All we like sheep have gone astray; we have turned—every one—to his own way; and the LORD has laid on him the iniquity of us all. (Isaiah 53:5–6)

Jesus's death also fulfilled Isaiah 53:10: "It was the will of the LORD to crush him; he has put him to grief; when his soul makes an offering for guilt . . . the will of the LORD shall prosper in his hand."

Near the end of his sixth hour on the cross, Jesus cried out in a loud voice, "My God, my God, why have you forsaken me?" This is an exact quote from the first verse of Psalm 22. To "give his life a ransom for many," Jesus was cut off from his eternal fellowship with God the Father. This was necessary in order to be a complete offering for our sins.

Jesus then spoke his fifth word from the cross: "I am thirsty" (John 19:28). He said this knowing that his work of redemption was accomplished. The Bible notes that Jesus said this in order to fulfill Scripture. Jesus understood that the Old Testament prophecies were fulfilled in him. However, it is also understandable that a man who had been scourged and nailed to the cross for six hours in the hot sun of Palestine would be extremely dehydrated. Intense thirst was a part of the torture. "A jar full of sour wine stood there, so they put a sponge full of the sour wine on a hyssop branch and held it to his mouth" (John 19:29). This fulfilled Psalm 69:21: "For my thirst they gave me sour wine to drink." This wine should not be confused with the wine mixed with myrrh that Jesus refused just before he was crucified. That was a sedative that would dull the pain. Jesus was determined to endure every aspect of God's justice to redeem sinners. What was given to Jesus now was a cheap wine the soldiers drank.

After Jesus had received the sour wine he said, "It is finished" (John 19:30). Jesus was not just saying his life was over. More importantly, he was stating that his work of redeeming sinners was completely accomplished. Jesus's last words on the cross were "'Father, into your hands I commit my spirit!' And having said this he breathed his last" (Luke 23:46). John adds an important point: "He bowed his head and gave up his spirit" (John 19:30). Jesus laid down his own life. This is in keeping with his prediction:

> For this reason the Father loves me, because I lay down my life that I may take it up again. No one takes it from me, but I lay it down of my own accord. I have authority to lay it down, and I have authority to take it up again. This charge I have received from my Father. (John 10:17–18)

Unusual Events Accompanying Jesus's Death

As soon as Jesus died, the curtain in the temple was torn in two from top to bottom (Matthew 27:51). The curtain in the temple separated the outer courts of the temple from the inner court, called the Holy of Holies. The curtain was made of white linen fabric, with blue, purple, and scarlet strands woven into it. These colors formed a picture of cherubim, the angels that guarded God's holiness. The curtain symbolized that the way into God's holy presence was not open to the general public (Exodus 26:31–35; 36:35; 2 Chronicles 3:14). God gave the exact pattern of the tabernacle (and the later temple) to Moses and commanded him to follow it. This inner court was the area that only the high priest would enter once a year on the Day of Atonement to offer sacrifices for the people of Israel. God would manifest his presence there, and even the high priest would be struck dead if he didn't follow the various cleansing rites and sacrifices God prescribed before he entered the Holy of Holies. Suddenly, though, the curtain was torn in two from top to bottom, showing that this was the work of God. The torn curtain symbolically points to the fact that Jesus's work on the cross was complete and that those who believe in him would now have direct access to God.

Another unusual event that took place at the time of Jesus's death was an earthquake. "The earth shook, and the rocks were split" (Matthew 27:51). This leads directly to the next event: tombs were opened because of the earthquake, and many bodies of past faithful believers were raised from the dead and, after Jesus's resurrection, went into Jerusalem, where many people saw them. Apparently they then went to heaven. This very unusual event prophetically points toward the future resurrection promised to all who believe in Jesus.

These events point to the great benefits believers in Jesus possess: direct access to God through the work of Jesus and an absence of fear of death because of the sure hope of being with God in heaven at death—and forever following the future resurrection of our bodies.

The centurion guarding Jesus during the crucifixion observed the darkness on the land and the light coming back just before he saw Jesus's giving up his spirit into the hands of his Father. He felt the earthquake at the time of Jesus's death. In seeing these things he was filled with awe and said, "Truly this was the Son of God!" (Matthew 27:54).

Events after Jesus's Death

This all took place in the middle of Friday afternoon. The Jewish Sabbath started at sunset, and the Jewish leaders were concerned about bodies left hanging all night on the crosses. In fact, this was a special Sabbath, since it was the week of Passover. At times those in the Sanhedrin were very scrupulous in obeying the ceremonial law of Moses. This is ironic, since they held an illegal trial of Jesus at night and brought false witnesses to testify against him. Deuteronomy 21:23 states that the land would be defiled if a body hung on a tree overnight. So the Jews asked Pilate if the legs of those being crucified might be broken in order to speed up their deaths. This was a common practice concerning those who were being crucified. The breaking of their legs with a hammer or iron bar made it impossible for those on a cross to push themselves up to breathe, and they would die quickly.

Pilate granted permission for this action. The soldiers broke the legs of the two thieves crucified with Jesus, apparently moving from the outside toward the middle, but when they came to Jesus they saw that he was dead already, so they did not break his legs (John 19:31–33). To ensure that Jesus was really dead, one of the Roman soldiers took a spear and thrust it into Jesus's side, and out came blood and water. However medical experts work out the meaning of this phenomenon, it emphasizes that Jesus was truly dead. This was a fulfillment of prophecy:

> One of the soldiers pierced his side with a spear, and at once there came out blood and water. He who saw it has borne witness—his testimony is true, and he knows that he is telling the truth— that you also may believe. For these things took place that the Scripture might be fulfilled: "Not one of his bones will be broken." And again another Scripture says, "They will look on him whom they have pierced." (John 19:34–37)

The direct Old Testament Scripture fulfilled here is Psalm 34:20. It is also important to note that, when God established the Passover feast, he told the Israelites not to break any of the bones of the Passover lamb (Exodus 12:46). This symbolically pointed toward Jesus's bones not being broken. Zechariah 12:10 was also fulfilled, for it speaks of people looking on the one they have pierced.

The Burial of Jesus

A man named Joseph, from the Jewish town of Arimathea, went to Pilate and asked for the body of Jesus. This was a courageous thing to do, for several reasons. First, according to Roman law those condemned to death lost the right to be buried. Second, Pilate hated the Jews and had just a short time before refused the request of Jewish leaders to change the inscription over Jesus that Pilate had written. Finally, the Bible informs us that Joseph was a member of the Sanhedrin, the Jewish ruling body, but had not consented to their actions concerning Jesus. Earlier, threats had been made by the leaders that anyone confessing Jesus was to be put out of their synagogue. In asking for Jesus's body, Joseph was confessing that he was a secret disciple of Jesus.

Pilate was surprised to hear that Jesus was already dead. It usually took much longer than six hours to die on a cross. He verified the information with the centurion and granted Joseph's request. Joseph, along with Nicodemus, who had come to Jesus earlier (John 3), brought a linen shroud and laid him in a tomb belonging to Joseph that had been cut out of rock. They prepared the body with about one hundred pounds of myrrh and aloes and bound it in linen bandages, as was the Jewish custom. They then rolled a stone in front of the tomb (John 19:38–42). Mary Magdalene and another Mary, described as the mother of Joses, saw where he was laid. This is important, because these women went to the same tomb on Sunday morning to finish preparing the body of Jesus. They knew exactly where it was. This fulfilled Isaiah's prophecy: "They made his grave with the wicked and a rich man in his death" (Isaiah 53:9). Jesus was crucified between two thieves (the wicked) but buried in a rich man's grave.

What Is My Reaction to Jesus on the Cross?

Jesus's death on the cross is so important that we have devoted two chapters to it. This chapter began with the heading "Jesus Makes Atonement for Sins." The last chapter included a heading titled "The Reaction of Various People to Jesus on the Cross." It is time to tie these two headings together.

"Atonement" means dealing with sin so as to put it away and gain forgiveness. Jesus made atonement for the sins of everyone who would trust him as Lord and Savior. God is holy and we are not. There is no way any of us could make atonement for ourselves. "If you, LORD, kept a record of sins, Lord, who could stand?" (Psalm 130:3).

"By grace you have been saved through faith. And this is not your own doing; it is the gift of God, not a result of works, so that no one may boast" (Ephesians 2:8–9).

Plainly, we can never make atonement for our sins. We need a Savior to rescue us. And that is exactly who Jesus Christ is. Before Christ's birth, God through an angel told Joseph to name him "Jesus, for he will save his people from their sins" (Matthew 1:21). Jesus made atonement for sinners by dying on the cross in our place. He did what we could never do.

The reaction of various people to Jesus on the cross was the same, with one exception. The scribes and Jewish rulers mocked and hated Jesus. The passersby ridiculed and taunted him. The soldiers mocked him. Even one of the men crucified with Jesus reviled him. All of these responses to Jesus were negative. But there was one exception: the other man crucified with Jesus repented of his sins and believed in Jesus, who promised him that he would be with Jesus in heaven.

How will you respond to Jesus?

PART 6

Prophecies of Jesus's Resurrection

18

Jesus's Resurrection, Part 1

J esus's death and resurrection are the heart of the good
news of salvation. If Jesus had not risen from the dead,
his life, though noble and exemplary, would have simply
ended in tragedy. Paul says that the resurrection declared
Jesus to be "the Son of God in power" (Romans 1:4).
The resurrection proclaims both Jesus's identity and his
victory over sin and death.

Jesus Predicted His Resurrection

In our study of Jesus's life, we saw that he predicted to
his disciples that he was going to be crucified but would
rise again from the dead on the third day. They did not
understand this until after his resurrection. The Jewish
leaders asked Jesus for a sign to prove he was from God.
On one occasion, he answered them, "An evil and adul-
terous generation seeks for a sign, but no sign will be

given to it except the sign of the prophet Jonah. For just as Jonah was three days and three nights in the belly of the great fish, so will the Son of Man be three days and three nights in the heart of the earth" (Matthew 12:39; see Jonah 1:17). Jesus also directly prophesied his death and resurrection.

> From that time Jesus began to show his disciples that he must go to Jerusalem and suffer many things from the elders and chief priests and scribes, and be killed, and on the third day be raised. (Matthew 16:21)

> The Son of Man is about to be delivered into the hands of men, and they will kill him, and he will be raised on the third day. (Matthew 17:22–23)

> See, we are going up to Jerusalem. And the Son of Man will be delivered over to the chief priests and scribes, and they will condemn him to death and deliver him over to the Gentiles to be mocked and flogged and crucified, and he will be raised on the third day. (Matthew 20:17–19)

These are not guesses but Jesus's specific prophecies about where and how he would be killed, who would instigate his death, and the fact that he would rise on the third day.

Jesus also predicted his resurrection in the Gospel of John. When asked by what sign he threw the money-changers out of the temple, he replied, "Destroy this temple, and in three days I will raise it up" (John 2:19). The Jews thought he was talking about the temple building in Jerusalem, which had taken forty-six years to build. "But Jesus was speaking about the temple of his body. When therefore he was raised from the dead, his disciples remembered that he had said this, and they believed the Scripture and the word that Jesus had spoken" (verses 21–22).

Jesus plainly said he would willingly lay down his life for his sheep and take it up again: "For this reason the Father loves me, because I lay down my life that I may take it up again. No one takes it from me, but I lay it down of my own accord" (John 10:17–18).

The Old Testament Predicted Jesus's Resurrection

The Old Testament also contains prophecies of Jesus's resurrection. Peter quoted a psalm of King David in his Pentecost sermon: "You will not abandon my soul to Sheol, or let your holy one see corruption" (Psalm 16:10). Then Peter explained:

> Brothers, I may say to you with confidence about the patriarch David that he both died and was buried, and his tomb is with us to this day. Being therefore a prophet, and knowing that God had sworn with an oath to him that he would set one of his descendants on his throne, he foresaw and

spoke about the resurrection of the Christ, that he was not abandoned to Hades, nor did his flesh see corruption. This Jesus God raised up, and of that we all are witnesses. (Acts 2:29–32)

The New Testament includes at least ten appearances of Jesus after his resurrection. Five took place on that first "Easter" and another five during the forty days until Jesus ascended into heaven. In this chapter we will explore Jesus's first five resurrection appearances.

The First Witnesses of the Resurrection

All four Gospels report that after the Saturday Sabbath was over, several women went to Jesus's tomb to anoint his body with spices they had prepared. While they were on their way, they wondered who would roll away the stone in front of the tomb for them (Mark 16:3). When they arrived at the tomb, they discovered that the guard was gone and the stone was already rolled back. There had been an earthquake, and an angel from heaven had rolled the stone away (Matthew 28:2). The women went into the tomb but did not find Jesus's body.

While they were perplexed, two angels dressed in dazzling apparel appeared and asked, "Why do you seek the living among the dead? He is not here, but has risen. Remember how he told you, while he was still in Galilee, that the Son of Man must be delivered into the hands of sinful men and be crucified and on the third day rise"

(Luke 24:5–7). The women remembered Jesus's words, returned from the tomb, and told his eleven disciples what they had seen and heard. When the women were on their way back, "Jesus met them and said, 'Greetings!' And they came up and took hold of his feet and worshiped him" (Matthew 28:8–9). This was his first post-resurrection appearance.

After the women reported these things to the apostles, Peter and John ran to the tomb; John outran Peter and arrived first. John stooped and looked into the tomb. Peter arrived and went into the tomb. He saw the face cloth that had been on Jesus's head; it was not with the other linen cloths but was folded up in a place by itself. Then John also went into the tomb and saw these things and believed (John 20:2–10). They both went home amazed at what had happened.

Jesus Appears to Mary Magdalene

Apparently, Mary Magdalene followed Peter and John back to the tomb but missed them when they returned a different way. As Mary stood weeping, she stooped to look into the tomb. She saw two angels in white, one sitting at the head and one at the feet of where Jesus's body had been (John 20:11–12). They asked Mary why she was weeping. She said that she thought someone had taken Jesus's body away. Then she turned and saw Jesus standing but didn't recognize him. Maybe tears blinded her or God kept her from recognizing Jesus. He asked her why she was crying. Mary thought he was the gardener and asked, "Sir, if you have carried him away, tell me where you have laid him." Jesus said to her, "Mary." She turned and called him "Teacher" (verses 15–16). Jesus told her not to cling to him, for he had not yet ascended to his Father. Mary went and told the disciples that she had seen the Lord, who had said these things to her.

Jesus Appears to Two on the Road to Emmaus

On the Sunday that Jesus arose, two men were walking to a village called Emmaus (seven miles from Jerusalem). As they walked, they talked about the events surrounding Jesus's death. Jesus walked up to them, but God kept them from recognizing him (Luke 24:13–16). He asked them what they were talking about. One of them, named Cleopas, asked him, "Are you the only visitor to Jerusalem who does not know the things that have happened there in these days?" (verse 18). When Jesus asked them what they were talking about, they answered:

> Concerning Jesus of Nazareth, a man who was a prophet mighty in deed and word before God and all the people and how our chief priests and rulers delivered him up to be condemned to death, and crucified him, but we had hoped that he was the one to redeem Israel. Yes, and besides all this, it is now the third day since these things happened. Moreover, some women of our company amazed

us. They were at the tomb early in the morning, and when they did not find his body, they came back saying that they had even seen a vision of angels, who said that he was alive. Some of those who were with us went to the tomb and found it just as the women had said, but him they did not see. (Luke 24:19–24)

Jesus replied, " 'O foolish ones, and slow of heart to believe all that the prophets have spoken! Was it not necessary that the Christ should suffer these things and enter into his glory?' And beginning with Moses and all the Prophets, he interpreted to them in all the Scriptures the things concerning himself" (Luke 24:25–27). All through our story of Jesus's life, we've observed many Old Testament prophecies that were fulfilled in the events of his life. Jesus pointed out many of these to the two men and explained the prophecies to them.

As they approached Emmaus, it was getting dark and the two men decided to wait until morning to finish their journey. Traveling late at night entailed various dangers, including difficulty in seeing the path, robbers, and wild animals. The men strongly urged Jesus to stay with them, and he did. As they ate, Jesus took the bread, blessed it, broke it, and began to give it to them. When he did so, their eyes were opened and they recognized him. At that moment he vanished from their sight (Luke 24:30–31). Apparently, Jesus's resurrection body possessed qualities that allowed him to vanish at will. "They said to each other, 'Did not our hearts burn within us while he talked to us on the road, while he opened to us the Scriptures?'" (Luke 24:32).

These men, dejected at the beginning of their journey, were now filled with hope and joy. They had assurance that Jesus had truly conquered death. They could not wait until the morning to tell others about meeting Jesus. They returned to Jerusalem, where the eleven told them, "'The Lord has risen indeed, and has appeared to Simon!' Then they told what had happened on the road, and how he was known to them in the breaking of the bread" (verses 33–35).

Jesus Appears to Ten Disciples in the Upper Room (Luke 24:36–49)

While the two men who had met Jesus on the road to Emmaus were telling their story, he appeared to the group. This group consisted of ten of Jesus's disciples, for Thomas was absent and Judas was dead. Jesus stood among them and said, "Peace to you!" They were frightened and thought they were seeing a spirit. He asked, "'Why are you troubled, and why do doubts arise in your hearts? See my hands and my feet, that it is I myself. Touch me, and see. For a spirit does not have flesh and bones as you see that I have.' And when he had said this, he showed them his hands and his feet" (Luke 24:38–40). Jesus then reinforced the fact that he had risen bodily from the dead by eating a piece of broiled fish in front of them (24:41–42). This was no hallucination. They all saw him and had physical evidence—the fish had been eaten!

Jesus then referred back to the times when he had prophesied to them that he was going to be crucified and would rise again on the third day: "These are my words that I spoke to you while I was still with you, that everything written about me in the Law of Moses and the Prophets and the Psalms must be fulfilled" (verse 44). (These are the three divisions of the Jewish Old Testament.) Just as he explained the Old Testament prophecies concerning his death and resurrection to the two men on the road to Emmaus, now he did the same to his disciples in the upper room: "Then he opened their minds to understand the Scriptures, and said to them, 'Thus it is written, that the Christ should suffer and on the third day rise from the dead, and that repentance and forgiveness of sins should be proclaimed in his name to all nations, beginning from Jerusalem. You are witnesses of these things'" (verses 45–48).

Jesus's Resurrection and Us

Jesus's death and resurrection are the two most important events in history. His atoning death is God's basis for forgiving the sins of anyone who believes in Jesus as Savior. As the Old Testament, Jesus himself, and his apostles predicted, after dying on the cross and being buried Jesus arose from the grave.

His resurrection has immediate and long-term benefits for believers. Everyone who trusts him as Savior moves from spiritual death to spiritual life with God now. This is because Jesus is alive to give eternal life to those who were dead in their sins. In mercy, God the Father "has caused us to be born again to a living hope through the resurrection of Jesus Christ from the dead" (1 Peter 1:3). Jesus's death and resurrection bring forgiveness of sins and eternal life to believers now. But there is more. As Jesus said, "Because I live you also will live" (John 14:19). This means that because of his resurrection we too will be raised from the dead on the last day to enjoy eternal life on the new earth with Jesus and all believers.

19

Jesus's Resurrection, Part 2

J esus's death and resurrection occupy center stage in
God's plan. In the last chapter we examined Jesus's
five resurrection appearances on the first "Easter." Here
we look at the remaining five.

Jesus Appears to the Disciples
Again with Thomas Present

When Jesus appeared to the disciples that first Sunday,
Thomas was absent, although we don't know why. The
other disciples told Thomas about seeing Jesus, but he
doubted Jesus's resurrection: "Unless I see in his hands
the mark of the nails, and place my finger into the mark
of the nails, and place my hand into his side, I will never
believe" (John 20:25). Thomas set forth the conditions
that would convince him that Jesus was alive. He must

see and touch Jesus, particularly the nail prints and the wound in his side left by the spear.

On the next Sunday Jesus appeared to them again, with Thomas present. Jesus spoke gently to Thomas and invited him to touch the nail prints and his side. Jesus did not rebuke Thomas but dealt tenderly with him. He encouraged Thomas not to disbelieve but to believe. Thomas then made a great statement to Jesus: "My Lord and my God!" This is one of the places in the New Testament where Jesus is directly called "God." Jesus didn't correct Thomas and say, "I know you're impressed, but I'm not God." Instead, Jesus accepted Thomas's confession and pronounced a blessing on him and future believers: "Have you believed because you have seen me? Blessed are those who have not seen and yet have believed" (John 20:29).

Jesus Appears to Seven of His Disciples by the Sea of Galilee

A little later Jesus appeared again to seven of his disciples by the Sea of Galilee. He had told them to meet him in Galilee, and some of them had arrived there. They still had to eat, and they went fishing. Because of the clear water in the Sea of Galilee, night was the best time for fishing. However, after fishing all night, they had not caught anything. Just as the day was breaking, Jesus stood on the shore and called, "Children, do you have any fish?" (John 21:5). They answered, "No." He told them to cast their net on the right side of the boat, where they would find fish. They did so and caught so many fish that they were not able to haul them in. This is a repetition of a miracle Jesus performed when he originally called his first disciples (Luke 5:1–11). John told Peter, "It is the Lord," and Peter jumped out of the boat and swam ashore. The rest of the disciples came in the boat, dragging the net full of fish (John 21:7–8).

When they came to the shore they saw a charcoal fire in place, with fish laid out on it, and bread. Jesus invited them to come and have breakfast with him. He also told them to bring some of the fish they had just caught. Peter went aboard the boat and dragged the net full of fish ashore. They counted them all: 153 fish. They then proceeded to have breakfast with Jesus.

After they had finished breakfast, Jesus turned to Peter and asked, "Simon, son of John, do you love me more than these?" Peter answered him, "Yes, Lord; you know that I love you." He said to him, "Feed my lambs." Jesus asked Peter a second time, "Simon, son of John, do you love me?" He replied, "Yes, Lord; you know that I love you." He said to him, "Tend my sheep." Jesus asked him a third time, "Simon, son of John, do you love me?" Peter was grieved that he had asked him the third time if he loved him. Peter remembered that he had denied Jesus three times during Jesus's trial. He answered Jesus, "Lord, you know everything; you know that I love you." Jesus said to him, "Feed my sheep" (John 21:15–17). In

this action Jesus restored Peter and called him to care for
and teach his people as an apostle.

Jesus Appears to His Disciples and Others on a Mountain in Galilee

Earlier Jesus had conveyed the message to his disciples to
meet him in Galilee. There he met with seven of the disciples, who had apparently arrived first by the Sea of Galilee. In this appearance he met with the eleven disciples
and most likely more than five hundred people at one
time on one of the hills in Galilee (1 Corinthians 15:6).
Matthew records this event:

> Now the eleven disciples went to Galilee, to the
> mountain to which Jesus had directed them. And
> when they saw him they worshiped him, but some
> doubted. And Jesus came and said to them, "All
> authority in heaven and on earth has been given
> to me. Go therefore and make disciples of all na-
> tions, baptizing them in the name of the Father
> and of the Son and of the Holy Spirit, teaching
> them to observe all that I have commanded you.
> And behold, I am with you always, to the end of
> the age." (Matthew 28:16–20)

In this meeting with his disciples and others, Jesus
gave important commands. He commissioned them to
go into the world and make disciples of all nations. They
were to baptize new disciples in the name of the Father,

the Son, and the Holy Spirit. They were to pass on Jesus's teachings. He also promised them that he would be with them in this task until his return. In this action Jesus commissioned his apostles, along with a large company of believers, to be faithful witnesses to him in the world. They were to be the beginning of the worldwide church. This is commonly called the Great Commission and is an important passage for evangelism and missions.

Jesus Appears to His Half-brother James

After this, during the forty days between Jesus's resurrection and ascension into heaven, he appeared to his disciples many times and proved to them that he had risen from the dead (Acts 1:3). Also sometime during this period he appeared to his half-brother James (1 Corinthians 15:7). Before Jesus's death and resurrection, "not even his brothers believed in him" (John 7:5). That changed when Jesus appeared to James after his resurrection, for he believed in Jesus. He became a leader among the Jewish Christians in the Jerusalem church (Acts 12:17; 15:3; Galatians 1:19) and wrote the letter bearing his name (James 1:1).

Jesus Appears to His Disciples at His Ascension

After he was raised from the dead, Jesus "presented himself alive to them after his suffering by many proofs, appearing to them during forty days and speaking about the kingdom of God" (Acts 1:3). This includes his being with them as he ascended into heaven (verse 9). Because we treat this in the next chapter, we only mention it here to round out our treatment of Jesus's ten post-resurrection appearances.

Solid Proofs upon Which to Build Our Faith

The resurrection of the Lord Jesus Christ sets apart Christianity from other world religions, for of all the founders of the world's religions, Jesus alone is alive. God the Father's raising Jesus from the dead set the Father's seal of approval on Jesus's atoning death. Jesus's death saves sinners because he is alive (1 Corinthians 15:17). His resurrection promises eternal life now to all who trust him as Lord and Savior. And because Jesus is alive and all-powerful, he will raise believers' bodies when he returns (verse 22; Philippians 3:20–21).

Scripture's many proofs of Jesus's resurrection are solid rocks upon which to build our faith. The New Testament presents at least ten appearances of Jesus after his resurrection, not counting the various times he appeared to his disciples in the forty days before his ascension.

(1) Jesus appeared first to the women who had left the empty tomb (Matthew 28:8–10).

(2) Then to Mary Magdalene, who had returned to the tomb after informing the disciples of what she and the women had seen there (Matthew 28:1–6).

(3) Jesus then appeared to Cleopas and his companion on the road to Emmaus (Luke 24:13–35).

(4) Then to Peter sometime that afternoon (Luke 24:34; 1 Corinthians 15:5).

(5) That evening Jesus appeared to the ten disciples in the upper room. Thomas was not there, and Judas was already dead (Luke 24:36–43).

(6) On the next Sunday he appeared again to his disciples with Thomas present. He invited Thomas to touch his nail prints and the place in his side pierced by the spear (John 20:26–29).

(7) A short time later Jesus appeared to seven of his disciples by the Sea of Galilee, where he had breakfast with them and restored Peter (John 21:1–22).

(8) Then he appeared to his eleven disciples on a mountain in Galilee (Matthew 28:16–20). This most likely was his appearance to more than five hundred disciples at once (1 Corinthians 15:6).

(9) At some point Jesus appeared to his half-brother James (1 Corinthians 15:7).

(10) Finally, he appeared to his disciples at the time of his ascension into heaven (Acts 1:4–9).

PART 7

Prophecies of Jesus's Ascension and Second Coming

20

Jesus's Ascension, Pentecost, and Second Coming

Jesus's life on earth began and ended with supernatural events. His earthly life began when he was conceived in his mother Mary's womb by the working of the Holy Spirit (Luke 1:35). The last event in the earthly life and ministry of Jesus was his ascension into heaven. Even after this he continued to work. In fulfillment of Old Testament prophecy he poured out the Holy Spirit on the church on the day of the Jewish festival of Pentecost. In heaven he continues to pray for believers, who await his return. Unlike his first coming, Jesus's second coming will be seen by all. In this chapter we will examine three events: Jesus's ascension, his pouring out of the Spirit at Pentecost, and his return.

Jesus Ascends to the Father

At the end of his Gospel Luke only briefly mentions that Jesus ascended into heaven, but the book of Acts elaborates on this event. It states that Jesus appeared to his disciples over forty days: "He presented himself alive to them after his suffering by many proofs, appearing to them during forty days and speaking about the kingdom of God" (Acts 1:3). The disciples asked Jesus if he was going to restore the kingdom to Israel at that time (verse 6). They may have been thinking of a political restoration. However, Jesus told them that the plans and timing of God were not for them to know; he directed their attention instead to the ministry he was calling them to perform.

After Jesus said these things he was lifted up and ascended toward heaven. The disciples watched this intently until Jesus disappeared behind a cloud. As the disciples were staring at the sky, two angels appeared in white robes and asked, "Men of Galilee, why do you stand looking into heaven? This Jesus, who was taken up from you into heaven, will come in the same way as you saw him go into heaven" (Acts 1:10–11). The angels were reiterating what Jesus had already taught his disciples: at the end of the age "they will see the Son of Man coming in a cloud with power and great glory" (Luke 21:27).

The Gospels anticipated Jesus's ascension. He made statements about himself that were hard for people to accept. The crowd had become hostile to Jesus because of his claims to be God and to be the only way to salvation. Jesus then asked questions that made it even harder for them to accept him: "Do you take offense at this? Then what if you were to see the Son of Man ascending to where he was before?" (John 6:61–62). Jesus's statement about his future ascension even increased their hostility, and many chose to leave him (verse 66).

After Jesus's resurrection, Mary and the other women came to the grave to prepare Jesus's body for burial. They found the tomb empty. Mary hurried back to tell the other disciples, and Peter and John ran to the tomb. Seeing the empty tomb, they returned to their homes. Mary stayed behind, weeping, thinking that someone had stolen Jesus's body. As Mary wept, she stooped to look into the tomb. She saw two angels, who asked her why she was weeping. She told them that someone had stolen Jesus's body. After she said this she turned around and saw Jesus standing there but did not know it was he. She told him the same thing about Jesus's body being stolen. He then said to her, "Mary." She immediately knew it was Jesus. He said to her, "Do not cling to me, for I have not yet ascended to the Father, but go to my brothers and say to them, 'I am ascending to my Father and your Father, to my God and your God'" (John 20:17). Jesus told her that his work would continue, but in a different way.

He had not come back permanently but would return to his Father in his ascension. The work of redemption would continue, but now in a different way: through the work of the Holy Spirit. Therefore, the ascension did not come out of the blue but was anticipated earlier in the Gospel accounts.

We can learn important lessons from this event. First, the angels said that Jesus would return the same way he left—visibly and bodily. Other passages in the New Testament teach the same thing. Jesus had warned his disciples that false teachers would come, claiming they were the returning Christ. "If they say to you, 'Look, he is in the wilderness,' do not go out. If they say, 'Look, he is in the inner rooms,' do not believe it. For as the lightning comes from the east and shines as far as the west, so will be the coming of the Son of Man" (Matthew 24:26–27). Jesus's return will be as visible as a huge lightning bolt in the sky. Second, Jesus told them it was not for human beings to know the time of his second coming: "Concerning that day and hour no one knows" (verse 36). Many false teachers in church history have claimed to know the exact time Jesus is going to return. Jesus speaks strongly against those teachers. Third, Jesus is now at the right hand of the Father, where he intercedes for his people. Peter made this application of the ascension in his sermon on the day of Pentecost, to which we now turn.

Jesus Pours Out the Holy Spirit at Pentecost

Long ago the Old Testament prophet Joel predicted, "It shall come to pass afterward, that I will pour out my Spirit on all flesh. . . . in those days I will pour out my Spirit" (Joel 2:28–29). Jesus fulfilled Joel's prophecy when he poured out the Holy Spirit on the church at Pentecost. In the Gospels Jesus promised that he would send the Holy Spirit to empower his disciples. In Acts 1:8 he told his disciples to wait in Jerusalem for this: "You will receive power when the Holy Spirit has come upon you, and you will be my witnesses in Jerusalem and in all Judea and Samaria, and to the end of the earth." This verse also provides an outline of the apostles' ministry that followed. Peter proclaimed that the power of the Holy Spirit the people were witnessing was a result of Jesus's ascension. Peter said that Jesus, having ascended to heaven, had poured out this Holy Spirit (Acts 2:33). Now Jesus rules from his royal throne in heaven. Even if the world is unwilling to acknowledge his identity or sovereignty, he is still reigning and ruling. One day he will finally put all his enemies under his feet upon his return.

Pentecost was a Jewish celebration that took place fifty days after Passover. Jewish people were gathered in Jerusalem from various places in the Roman Empire. The disciples and other followers of Jesus were gathered in an upper room when the Holy Spirit came upon them, as Jesus had promised. They supernaturally spoke in the languages of the various people gathered in Jerusalem, praising God in these languages. This caught the attention of the crowd, and Peter powerfully presented the gospel to them. In his sermon Peter tied an Old Testament prophecy to Jesus's ascension. Peter told them that the signs the people were witnessing were a confirmation from God that Jesus was the Messianic king who had fulfilled the promises to David that one of his descendants would have an eternal kingdom. Peter quoted and applied Psalm 110:1, a psalm of David:

> This Jesus God raised up, and of that we all are witnesses. Being therefore exalted at the right hand of God, and having received from the Father the promise of the Holy Spirit, he has poured out this that you yourselves are seeing and hearing. For David did not ascend into the heavens, but he himself says, "The Lord said to my Lord, Sit at my right hand, until I make your enemies your footstool." Let all the house of Israel therefore know for certain that God has made him both Lord and Christ, this Jesus whom you crucified. (Acts 2:32–36)

Peter concluded his speech with a call for faith and repentance, and about three thousand people came to faith in Jesus.

Peter's Pentecost sermon shows that Jesus's ascension was a confirmation that he was the fulfillment of the prophecy in Psalm 110:1. This prophecy was that one of David's descendants would be the Messianic king and fulfill all the promises to David. God made a covenant with David that his throne would be established forever. His dynasty lasted around four hundred years, a long time for an Old-Testament-era dynasty. However, it was not forever. Eventually in Old Testament history that dynasty ended. The promise is fulfilled in Jesus, a descendant of David according to his human nature (see Romans 1:3). The promise was fulfilled in the ascension of Jesus as he took his place ruling at the right hand of God.

Jesus Will Come Again

The Old Testament makes many predictions of Jesus's first coming but few of his second coming. Yet every part of the New Testament makes such prophecies, beginning with Jesus himself. In the Gospels he predicts his return when he refers to himself as the "Son of Man," his favorite self-designation:

> When the Son of Man comes in his glory, and all the angels with him, then he will sit on his glorious throne. Before him will be gathered all the nations, and he will separate people one from another as a shepherd separates the sheep from the goats. And he will place the sheep on his right, but the goats on the left. Then the King will say to those on his right, "Come, you who are blessed

by my Father, inherit the kingdom prepared for
you from the foundation of the world." (Matthew
25:31–34)

In John's Gospel Jesus comforts his disciples and all believers since then:

Let not your hearts be troubled. Believe in
God; believe also in me. In my Father's house are
many rooms. If it were not so, would I have told
you that I go to prepare a place for you? And if I
go and prepare a place for you, I will come again
and will take you to myself, that where I am you
may be also. (John 14:1–3)

The book of Acts also contains prophecies of Jesus's
second coming. While the disciples watched Jesus ascend,
two angels (like men in appearance) said that Jesus would
come again:

When he had said these things, as they were looking on, he was lifted up, and a cloud took him out
of their sight. And while they were gazing into
heaven as he went, behold, two men stood by
them in white robes, and said, "Men of Galilee,
why do you stand looking into heaven? This Jesus,
who was taken up from you into heaven, will
come in the same way as you saw him go into
heaven." (Acts 1:9–11)

The apostle Paul wrote on many themes in his letters, including the return of Christ to bless his people and judge the lost:

> Our citizenship is in heaven, and from it we await a Savior, the Lord Jesus Christ, who will transform our lowly body to be like his glorious body, by the power that enables him even to subject all things to himself. (Philippians 3:20–21)

> God considers it just to repay with affliction those who afflict you, and to grant relief to you who are afflicted as well as to us, when the Lord Jesus is revealed from heaven with his mighty angels in flaming fire, inflicting vengeance on those who do not know God and on those who do not obey the gospel of our Lord Jesus. They will suffer the punishment of eternal destruction, away from the presence of the Lord and from the glory of his might, when he comes on that day to be glorified in his saints, and to be marveled at among all who have believed. (2 Thessalonians 1:6–10)

Among the eight general epistles are the books of Hebrews, 1 Peter, and 1 John. These also predict the second coming:

> He has appeared once for all at the end of the ages to put away sin by the sacrifice of himself. And just as it is appointed for man to die once, and after

that comes judgment, so Christ, having been offered once to bear the sins of many, will appear a second time, not to deal with sin but to save those who are eagerly waiting for him. (Hebrews 9:26–28)

Preparing your minds for action, and being sober-minded, set your hope fully on the grace that will be brought to you at the revelation of Jesus Christ. (1 Peter 1:13)

Beloved, we are God's children now, and what we will be has not yet appeared; but we know that when he appears we shall be like him, because we shall see him as he is. And everyone who thus hopes in him purifies himself as he is pure. (1 John 3:2–3)

The very last book of the Bible, the book of Revelation, joins the other witnesses in proclaiming that Jesus will have a second coming:

I saw heaven opened, and behold, a white horse! The one sitting on it is called Faithful and True, and in righteousness he judges and makes war. His eyes are like a flame of fire, and on his head are many diadems, and he has a name written that no one knows but himself. He is clothed in a robe dipped in blood, and the name by which he is called is The Word of God. And the armies of heaven, arrayed in fine linen, white and pure, were following him on white horses. From his mouth comes a sharp sword with which to strike down the nations, and he will rule them with a rod of iron. He will tread the winepress of the fury of the wrath of God the Almighty. On his robe and on his thigh he has a name written, King of kings and Lord of lords. (Revelation 19:11–16)

In fact, near the very end of the book of Revelation, Jesus Christ himself speaks and promises to return to save all who "wash their robes," which means to trust in his blood (his death on the cross) to make them right with God: "Behold, I am coming soon, bringing my recompense with me, to repay everyone for what he has done. . . . Blessed are those who wash their robes, so that they may have the right to the tree of life" (Revelation 22:12, 14).

Connecting the Dots

Once more we see major events in Jesus's life predicted in Scripture. King David and Jesus himself predicted his ascension. The Old Testament prophet Joel prophesied that the Messiah (the Christ) would pour out the Spirit on God's people. This happened on the day of Pentecost. Jesus and his apostles predicted his second coming to bless his people and judge the lost. If you have read this far in this book and know that you are among the lost, we plead with you: believe in Jesus for salvation. Turn away from any efforts to save yourself and place all your faith for salvation in Jesus's death and resurrection. If you do so sincerely, God will forgive you of your sins and grant you the gift of eternal life.

Perhaps you are already a believer in Jesus but have drifted away from God and his Word. We urge you to read the Bible daily, for, as Jesus said, "Man shall not live by bread alone, but by every word that comes from the mouth of God" (Matthew 4:4, quoting Deuteronomy 8:3). We encourage you to desire the milk of the Word of God so that you will grow spiritually: "Like newborn infants, long for the pure spiritual milk, that by it you may grow up into salvation" (1 Peter 2:2). And if you have drifted away from the fellowship of God's people, we urge you, "Do not neglect to meet together, as is the habit of some, but encourage one another, and all the more as you see the Day [of Christ's return] drawing near" (Hebrews 10:25).

21

Conclusion

J im Carmichael tells his story of coming to faith in Jesus:

> I joined the Marine Corps when I was in high
> school, in February 1967. The war in Southeast
> Asia was raging, and I wanted to be part of help-
> ing that tiny nation defend itself against Com-
> munist aggression. I saw no need to reach out to
> God, because I was nineteen and invincible. Un-
> fortunately, I witnessed a lot of invincible kids die.
> War has a way of exposing every human weakness
> and revealing the most horrible sights and events.
> It also places young men and women in unwinna-
> ble situations that haunt combatants. Research
> tells us that combat changes people's brains to the
> point that they are too often transformed into an-
> gry and hopeless individuals. That is how I rotated
> home in December 1968.

It didn't take long before I realized something in me was wrong. As an angry combat Marine, I argued with my wife, not to prove I was right about everything but because I was in so much mental pain. By 1972, Catherine and I had separated and were probably headed toward divorce. That was when God intervened. He sent a man at my wife's workplace to share the gospel with her, and he suggested that we visit a church not far from our house. The pastor of that church came to visit and shared the plan of salvation with us, and we both trusted in Jesus for forgiveness and salvation. However, that same day my wife asked me to leave and go live somewhere else, which I did. This was not how I envisioned God's turning my life around for the better. However, it wasn't long before we got back together.

Through this event God manifested himself to our family. We both joined that small church and started to grow in our faith. However, my combat experiences were still affecting our marriage negatively. I would come home and, many times, lie on the floor and stare at the ceiling. I had nothing to give my wife after work. I was miserable most of the time. I couldn't explain what was wrong because I didn't know what was wrong. I would often get angry and stay that way for hours, sometimes for days.

God led us to Bible college and then seminary, but the war still had its grip on me despite the great teaching I had been given. We received a call to pastor a church in the upper Midwest in 1995, which we accepted. But after three-plus years I was admitted to the psychiatric ward at the local veterans' hospital, where I was diagnosed with PTSD (Post-Traumatic Stress Disorder). Now I understood the issue. I still struggle with my combat trauma, but God has taught my wife and me how to live with it by grace. Becoming a Christian doesn't mean healing of every kind. It does mean spiritual healing of the soul through forgiveness, righteousness, and the indwelling Holy Spirit, who applies the finished work of Christ to a person's life.

Jim Carmichael has taught with different mission groups in Ukraine, Haiti, India, and Mexico. He also has a ministry to veterans suffering from PTSD. His honest story dispels the myth that, once people come to know the Lord, their struggles and problems are over. This is a lie; the truth is that believers struggle like everyone else, but they have Jesus and his resources available to help them in time of need (Hebrews 4:14–16).

Let us review Jesus's story as told by an angel. Of course, we use our imagination and make believe that an angel tells the story, but the story he tells is true to Scripture.

Jesus's Life Told by the Angel Gabriel

I am an angel of the Lord named Gabriel, and I will tell you the story of Jesus.

Before Jesus's Birth

I was busy before Jesus was born. First, I appeared to John the Baptist's father, Zechariah, when, as a priest, he burned incense in the temple. Even though he and his wife were advanced in years, I told him that God would give them a son, whom they were to name John. I said that he would be a great man and would "turn many of the children of Israel to the Lord their God" (Luke 1:16). I introduced myself: "I am Gabriel. I stand in the presence of God, and I was sent to speak to you and to bring you this good news" (verse 19). Though Zechariah was slow to believe, the birth happened just as I said, and, when grown, John the Baptist prepared the way for Jesus.

Second, I appeared to Jesus's mother, Mary, and told her that she would give birth to the holy Son of God. When she asked how this could happen since she was a virgin, I explained that God would cause her to conceive a child through the Holy Spirit. I also told her to name her son Jesus, "the Lord saves," because that is exactly what he would do. Mary humbly submitted to God, and things happened as I had predicted. The Son of God became a baby boy who grew up to be the Savior of the world!

When Jesus was born in Bethlehem, we angels appeared to shepherds watching their flocks in the fields. It was nighttime, and God's glory shone brightly (Luke 2:9). At first only one of us appeared and told them the great news: "Unto you is born this day in the city of David a Savior, who is Christ the Lord" (verse 11). Suddenly a vast army of angels appeared, praising God: "Glory to God in the highest, and on earth peace among those with whom he is pleased!" (verse 14). We left, and the shepherds went to see the Christ child.

After Jesus Grew Up

When Jesus grew up and began his ministry, we angels ministered to him after his terrible forty days in the wilderness and his temptations by the devil (Matthew 4:11). Then followed Jesus's amazing three-and-a-half-year public ministry. It was not God's will for us to have a part in this. He did not need our help to preach about the kingdom of heaven, heal the sick, or cast out demons.

Jesus did mention us angels a few times in his teaching and parables. He spoke of the importance of not being ashamed to trust him as Lord and Savior: "Everyone who acknowledges me before men, the Son of Man also will acknowledge before the angels of God, but the one who denies me before men will be denied before the angels of God" (Luke 12:8–9). He let humans know that we good angels dwell in God's presence: "Just so, I tell you, there is joy before the angels of God over one sinner who repents" (Luke 15:10). Jesus meant that God rejoices over people coming to know him.

Sometimes people misunderstand Jesus's words. One example is when Jesus said of believers, "They cannot die anymore, because they are equal to angels and are sons of God, being sons of the resurrection" (Luke 20:36). Some think this means that, when humans die, they become angels. This is incorrect. God created angels as spiritual beings. We never have been or will be humans. Jesus's words mean that God will raise believers from the grave never to die again. In that way they will resemble us angels, who do not experience death.

When Jesus Dies, Rises, and Ascends

Jesus died on the cross in the place of human sinners because of his great love for them. He did not die for angels (Hebrews 2:14–16). This fulfilled prophecies, as did Jesus's resurrection. He rose triumphantly from the grave, defeating his enemies: Satan, evil angels, sin, death, and hell. Although we good angels had no part to play in Jesus's death, we were witnesses of his resurrection. Jesus died on Friday, and when women came on Sunday to see the tomb where his body was buried, "Behold, there was a great earthquake, for an angel of the Lord descended from heaven and came and rolled back the stone and sat on it. His appearance was like lightning, and his clothing white as snow" (Matthew 28:2–3). The angel calmed the women's fear: "Do not be afraid, for I know that you seek Jesus who was crucified. He is not here, for he has risen, as he said" (verses 5–6). Then the women believed and ran to tell Jesus's disciples, as the angel instructed.

We angels were involved when Jesus went back to heaven. When Jesus ascended in front of his disciples, they continued to gaze into heaven after a cloud had taken him away. Two angels, appearing as "two men" who "stood by them in white robes," asked, "Men of Galilee, why do you stand looking into heaven? This Jesus, who was taken up from you into heaven, will come in the same way as you saw him go into heaven" (Acts 1:11).

And then the most amazing thing happened: God the Father welcomed his beloved Son back into heaven. At that moment the Father said, "Let all God's angels worship him" (Hebrews 1:6). And that is what we did!

When Jesus Comes Again

Jesus explained that angels will perform certain jobs when he returns. We angels will accompany Jesus when he comes again, as he said: "When the Son of Man comes in his glory, and all the angels with him, then he will sit on his glorious throne" (Matthew 25:31). Jesus also taught that "at the end of the age the angels will come out and separate the evil from the righteous" (13:39). Make no mistake: Jesus came to save people from God's judgment. For this reason he spoke the most about hell in Scripture.

He did so because he came to deliver people from hell and wanted to warn them so they would believe in him and be saved.

Jesus left no doubt what unsaved people will experience, for he himself will tell the unsaved, "Depart from me, you cursed, into the eternal fire prepared for the devil and his angels" (Matthew 25:41). God created all us angels good in the beginning. But one angel led a rebellion of many angels who turned away from the Lord. They are evil angels and demons, and God has reserved a place in hell for them and their leader, the devil or Satan (Revelation 20:10).

As I said, we angels did not help Jesus during his earthly ministry. But we had roles to play toward the all-important end of his time on earth. Just before his disciple Judas betrayed him, Jesus prayed, asking his Father if it was possible for Jesus to be spared from dying on the cross. The Father said no to Jesus's request, and Jesus submitted to his will. "And there appeared to him an angel from heaven, strengthening him" (Luke 22:43).

Judas the betrayer came with "a great crowd with swords and clubs" to seize Jesus. Then his disciples began to fight to prevent his arrest. But Jesus stopped them and asked, "Do you think that I cannot appeal to my Father, and he will at once send me more than twelve legions of angels? But how then should the Scriptures be fulfilled, that it must be so?" (Matthew 26:53–54). We were ready to come to Jesus's aid at this crucial time, but it was not

God's will. Jesus knew that he had to go to the cross to fulfill God's plan and Old Testament prophecies.

Jesus's Purpose in Coming to Earth

Jesus's was the most amazing life ever lived. We angels were privileged to play a small part in it. But the whole purpose of his coming was to "seek and to save . . . lost" human beings (Luke 19:10). We worship God for his beautiful salvation of humans but do not understand as they do because we do not experience that salvation (1 Peter 1:12). We angels urge all humans to acknowledge their sin against God and to trust Jesus for salvation. Praise the name of Jesus!

Jesus's Life Fulfilled Many Old Testament Prophecies

We have told the story of Jesus's life from before his birth to his second coming. But this book's main point is that Jesus's life fulfilled a great number of Old Testament prophecies. Appendix 2 will list all the prophecies we treated, with Old Testament predictions and New Testament fulfillments. Here we list them to show the large number of predictions. Note that they spanned Jesus's whole life.

Prophecies of Jesus's Birth

Birthplace: Bethlehem

Early witnesses: Simeon and Anna

Visit from the Magi

Prophecies of the Beginning of Jesus's Ministry

The forerunner: John the Baptist

Temptations by Satan

Prophecies of the Heart of Jesus's Ministry

The raising of Lazarus

The healing of the sick

The casting out of demons

Prophecies of the End of Jesus's Ministry

Jesus's predictions of his death and resurrection

The triumphal entry

The Last Supper

Prayer in Gethsemane

Jesus's trials

Prophecies of Jesus's Death

The betrayal, arrest, and Peter's denial

The crucifixion

Prophecies of Jesus's Resurrection

Jesus's resurrection

Prophecies of Jesus's Ascension, Pentecost, and Second Coming

Jesus's Ascension

Jesus will pour out the Spirit at Pentecost

Jesus's Second Coming

God wanted us to understand that he predicted the major events in the life, death, and resurrection of Jesus. Why? First, God wanted to direct our attention to the importance of his beloved Son. Jesus is utterly unique. From all eternity he existed as God the Son in heaven with the Father and the Holy Spirit. Then, on the first Christmas, he became a human being just like us, except for sin. God prophesied so much concerning Jesus's life because Jesus is the only Savior of the world, as he said: "I am the way, and the truth, and the life. No one comes to the Father except through me" (John 14:6).

Second, God predicted so many events in Jesus's life, including his death and resurrection, because he wanted to inspire our confidence in his holy Word. Of all the books of the world's religions, only Christianity includes this feature of prediction and fulfillment. God hereby gave evidence of his existence and work in the world. He spoke through prophets, worked to fulfill their predictions in history, and moved New Testament writers to record these fulfillments. God did all this so that we would trust in the truthfulness and reliability of his Word. Scripture speaks truth, including when it tells us of Jesus's death in the place of us sinners. Scripture speaks truth when it tells of Jesus's triumphant resurrection that assures eternal life now and forever for all who trust Jesus as Lord and Savior. Do you?

Here is a true story of a man who thought he was too bad for Jesus to save. As I (Van) was growing up, my father owned a grocery store. I worked in this store as a teenager, stocking shelves and carrying groceries to people's cars. I regularly carried the groceries of an older man named Jimmy. Jimmy was a jovial man who liked to tell jokes. However, I noticed there seemed to be an underlying sadness in Jimmy at those times when he wasn't joking around. As a Christian young man, I spoke to Jimmy about the gospel and the promise of forgiveness through faith in Jesus. Jimmy looked extra sad and said, "No, I'm too bad to come to God." I told him that no one was too bad to come to Jesus, but he insisted all the more that he was too bad to ever be forgiven or to come to God. My dad also spoke to Jimmy about Jesus, with the same response.

One day my father and I invited Jimmy and his wife to an evangelistic meeting in our area. We were pleased that he and his wife went with us. The evangelist presented an illustration of the gospel that helped Jimmy. He said, "You can't drive a car looking in the rear-view mirror." He applied this to promises in the Bible that assure us that those who believe in Jesus are truly forgiven and accepted by God. Jimmy said that this really spoke to him, and he came to faith in Jesus. His wife did also. They were both extremely joyful, and Jimmy had an air of relief about him.

A few years later Jimmy had a heart attack. My father went to see him in the hospital. Jimmy told him about his past. He said, "When I was a young man back in the

1930s, I was involved with a gang that robbed a bank. There was a big shootout and a guard was killed. No one could tell whose bullet actually killed the man, but I think it was my shot that killed him. I went to prison for the attempted robbery, but I'm sure that I killed a man. For years I thought I was so bad as a murderer that I could never be forgiven. However, when I believed in Jesus I understood that because of Jesus's death and resurrection God could forgive even my sin. All through those years I knew that if I died, I would go to hell. When I had this heart attack I had peace because I knew for sure that if I died, I was going to heaven. I know I'm at peace with God through the work of Jesus."

Jimmy summarized well the great hope and comfort of the gospel. The apostle Paul wrote to the Corinthians:

> Now I would remind you, brothers, of the gospel I preached to you, which you received, in which you stand, and by which you are being saved, if you hold fast to the word I preached to you—unless you believed in vain. For I delivered to you as of first importance what I also received: that Christ died for our sins in accordance with the Scriptures, that he was buried, that he was raised on the third day in accordance with the Scriptures . . . (1 Corinthians 15:1–4)

You may not have a dramatic event in your past like Jimmy, but the Bible says that we "all have sinned and fall short of the glory of God" (Romans 3:23). True faith is a reliant trust in Jesus alone. We trust that Jesus accomplished everything needed for our salvation when he died and rose. When we transfer our trust from anything in ourselves to Jesus alone, God promises to forgive and accept us. Jimmy did this and knew that he was truly forgiven. If you've never done this, we urge you to believe in Jesus's death and resurrection to save you. Trust in him and receive his mercy and forgiveness.

Appendix 1: Outline of Jesus's Life

EVENTS IN JESUS'S LIFE	SCRIPTURE PASSAGE
Birth in Bethlehem	Matthew 1:18–25; Luke 2:1–7
Visit of shepherds and, later, Magi	Luke 2:8–20
Witness of Simeon and Anna	Luke 2:25–38
John the Baptist, Jesus's forerunner	Luke 3:1–20
Temptation by the devil	Matthew 4:1–11
Healing miracles	Matthew 15:30–31; John 9:1–41
Teaching	Matthew 5–7, 24–25
Parables	Matthew 13:1–52
Exorcisms	Matthew 8:28–34; Mark 5:8–13
Transfiguration	Matthew 17:1–8
Raising of Lazarus	John 11:1–44
Triumphal Entry	Matthew 21:1–11
Last Supper	Matthew 26:17–29

EVENTS IN JESUS'S LIFE	SCRIPTURE PASSAGE
Prayer in Gethsemane	Matthew 26:36–46
Betrayal by Judas	Matthew 26:47–56
Arrest	Matthew 26:47–56
Denial by Peter	Matthew 26:69–75
Trials	Matthew 26:57–68; 27:1–2; Luke 23:6–25; John 18:12–40
Death on the cross	Matthew 27:32–44
Resurrection	Matthew 28:1–10
Ascension	Acts 1:6–11
Pouring out of the Spirit at Pentecost	Acts 2:1–36
Second Coming	Still to come

Appendix 2:
Prophecies Treated in *Jesus in Prophecy*

EVENT	OLD TESTAMENT PROPHECY	FULFILLMENT
Introduction		
Plundering the Egyptians	Genesis 15:13–14	Exodus 12:35–36
Babylonian captivity of 70 years	Jeremiah 25:11	2 Kings 25:1–12
Destruction of Babylon	Jeremiah 25:12	Daniel 5
Messiah will be born in Bethlehem	Micah 5:2	Matthew 2:4–6
Messiah will be born of a virgin	Isaiah 7:14	Matthew 1:20–23
Messiah will preach gospel freedom	Isaiah 61:1–2	Luke 4:16–21
Messiah will die in the place of sinners	Isaiah 53:5	1 Peter 2:24
Messiah will rise from the dead	Psalm 16:8–11	Acts 2:24–28
Messiah will pour out the Spirit	Joel 2:28–29	Acts 2:16–18
Chapter 1: Jesus's Birth in Bethlehem		
Messiah will be born of a virgin	Isaiah 7:14	Matthew 1:20; Luke 1:35
David's descendant will rule forever	2 Samuel 7:12–13; Isaiah 9:6–7	Luke 1:32–33
Messiah will be born in Bethlehem	Micah 5:2	Luke 2:1–5

EVENT	PROPHECY	FULFILLMENT
Chapter 2: Jesus's Early Witnesses		
Simeon would see the Messiah	Luke 2:25–26	Luke 2:29–32
Messiah will be a light to the Gentiles	Isaiah 42:6; 49:6; 52:10	Luke 2:29–32
Messiah will divide	Luke 2:34–35	Matthew 10:34–36
Chapter 3: Jesus's Visit from the Magi		
Messiah will be born in Bethlehem	Micah 5:2	Matthew 2:4–6
"Out of Egypt I called my son"	Hosea 11:1	Matthew 2:13–15
Chapter 4: Jesus's Forerunner		
John the Baptist to go before Jesus	Isaiah 40:3–4, 6	Luke 3:4–6
Chapters 5: Jesus's Temptations		
"Man shall not live by bread alone"	Deuteronomy 8:3	Matthew 4:4
"You shall not put the Lord your God to the test"	Deuteronomy 6:16	Matthew 4:7
"You shall worship the Lord your God and him only shall you serve"	Deuteronomy 6:13	Matthew 4:10
Chapter 6: Jesus's Miracles		
Raising the dead	Isaiah 61:1–3	Luke 7:11–17; Matthew 9:23–26; John 11:1–44

EVENT	OLD TESTAMENT PROPHECY	FULFILLMENT
Chapter 7: Jesus's Exorcisms		
Healing a man born blind	Isaiah 42:1, 5–7	John 9:1–41
Chapter 8: Jesus's Raising of Lazarus		
Freeing demon-possessed men	Isaiah 61:1	Mark 5:8–13

JESUS'S PREDICTION	PASSAGE	FULFILLMENT
Chapter 9: Jesus's Predictions of His Death &Resurrection		
Jews will reject their Messiah	Matthew 23:37–38	Matthew 27:22–23
A disciple will betray Jesus	Matthew 26:20–25	Matthew 26:47–56
Jesus will be arrested, die, and rise	Matthew 16:21; 17:22–23; 20:18–19	Matthew 26:50; 27:50; 28:6
Jesus will come again	Matthew 24:30–31	Still future
Last judgment will occur	Matthew 25:31–36	Still future
Final kingdom of God will come	Matthew 19:28	Still future
Temple will be destroyed	Matthew 24:2	Romans in A.D. 70

EVENT	OLD TESTAMENT PROPHECY	FULFILLMENT
Chapter 10: Jesus's Triumphal Entry		
Jesus will ride donkey into Jerusalem	Zechariah 9:9; Isaiah 62:11	Matthew 21:5; John 12:14–15

EVENT	PROPHECY	FULFILLMENT
Prediction of Jerusalem's destruction	Luke 19:42–44	Romans in A.D. 70

JESUS'S PREDICTION	PASSAGE	FULFILLMENT
Chapter 11: Jesus's Last Supper		
A disciple will betray him	Matthew 26:20–25; Psalm 41:9; John 13:18–19	Matthew 26:47–56
Disciples will fall away	Zechariah 13:7; Matthew 26:31	Matthew 26:56
Peter will deny him	Matthew 26:33–34	Matthew 26:69–75
Chapter 12: Jesus's Prayer in Gethsemane		
Disciples will fall away	Zechariah 13:7; Matthew 26:31	Matthew 26:56
Jesus will rise from the dead	Matthew 26:32	Matthew 28:6
Peter will deny him	Matthew 26:33–34	Matthew 26:69–75
Disciples will fail and return	Luke 22:32	Matthew 26:56; Matthew 28:16–20

EVENT	OLD TESTAMENT PROPHECY	FULFILLMENT
Chapter 13: Jesus's Betrayal, Arrest, & Denial		
Messiah will be betrayed for thirty pieces of silver	Zechariah 11:12	Matthew 26:15
Jesus predicts disciples will fall away	Zechariah 13:7	Matthew 26:56

EVENT	PROPHECY	FULFILLMENT
Prediction of Peter's denial	Luke 22:34	Matthew 26:69–75
Chapter 14: Jesus's Trials, Part 1		
Jesus will be silent before accusers	Isaiah 53:7	Matthew 26:62–63a
Jesus is the Son of Man	Daniel 7:13–14	Mark 14:62
Chapter 15: Jesus's Trials, Part 2		
Prediction of his crucifixion	John 18:32	John 19:18
Messiah will not sin	Isaiah 53:9	Peter 2:22
Chapter 16: Jesus's Crucifixion, Part 1		
Messiah will be scourged	Isaiah 53:5	Matthew 27:26
Jerusalem will be destroyed	Luke 23:28–31	Romans in A.D. 70
Messiah will be offered sour wine	Psalm 69:20–21	Matthew 27:34
Messiah will be crucified between robbers	Isaiah 53:9–12	Matthew 27:38
Messiah will ask God to forgive enemies	Isaiah 53:12	Luke 23:34; Acts 2:37–47; 4:4; 6:7
Soldiers will cast lots for Messiah's tunic	Psalm 22:18	John 19:23–24
People will ridicule and taunt Messiah	Psalm 22:6–8; Isaiah 37:22–23	Matthew 27:39–43

EVENT	PROPHECY	FULFILLMENT
Chapter 17: *Jesus's Crucifixion, Part 2*		
Jesus will give his life as a ransom	Isaiah 53:5–6	Mark 10:45
Jesus's body will be broken and blood spilt	Isaiah 53:10	Matthew 26:26–28
"My God, why have you forsaken me?"	Psalm 22:1	Matthew 27:46
Messiah will be thirsty and drink	Psalm 69:21	John 19:29
Messiah will lay down his own life	John 10:17–18	John 19:30
None of Messiah's bones will be broken	Psalm 34:20	John 19:34–37
Messiah's body will be pierced	Zechariah 12:10	John 19:34–37
Messiah's grave will made with a rich man	Isaiah 53:9	John 19:41–42
Chapter 18: *Jesus's Resurrection, Part 1*		
Jonah as a type of Jesus's resurrection	Jonah 1:17 Matthew 12:39	Matthew 28:5–6
Jesus's prediction of his resurrection	Matthew 16:21; 17:22–23; 20:17–19; John 2:19; 10:17–18	Luke 24:5–7 John 2:20–22

EVENT	PROPHECY	FULFILLMENT
Resurrection foretold in Psalms	Psalm 16:10	Acts 2:29–32
Resurrection foretold in Old Testament	Luke 24:25–27, 44–46	Luke 24:6
Chapter 20: Jesus's Ascension, Pentecost, & Second Coming		
Angels predict return at ascension	Acts 1:10–11	Acts 1:9
Jesus predicts his return	Luke 21:27; Matthew 4:26–27	Still future
Jesus predicts his ascension	John 6:61–62; 20:17	Acts 1:9
Messiah will pour out the Holy Spirit	Joel 2:28–29	Acts 2:33
The Holy Spirit will come	Acts 1:8	Acts 2:33
Messiah will sit at God's right hand	Psalm 110:1	Acts 2:32–36
Jesus predicts his return	Matthew 25:31–34; John 14:1–3; Revelation 22:12, 14	Still future
Paul predicts Jesus's return	Philippians 3:20–21; 2 Thessalonians 1:6–10	Still future
Other apostles predict Jesus's return	Hebrews 9:26–28; 1 Peter 1:13; 1 John 3:2–3; Revelation 19:11–16	Still future

Appendix 3:
Prophecies Made by Jesus

PROPHECY	PASSAGE
Jesus prophesied that the Gentiles would believe in him while many Jews would reject him.	Matthew 8:10–12; 23:37–38
Jesus foretold one of his disciples would betray him.	Matthew 26:20–25
Jesus foretold his death by crucifixion.	John 18:31–32
On three different occasions Jesus foretold his arrest, death, and resurrection.	(1) Matthew 16:21; Mark 8:31; Luke 9:22; (2) Matthew 17:22–23; Mark 9:31; Luke 9:44; (3) Matthew 20:18–19; Mark 10:33–34; Luke 18:32–33
Jesus predicted his resurrection.	John 2:19–22
Jesus foretold that his disciples would be persecuted as they bore witness to him to both Jews and Gentiles.	Matthew 10:16–20

PROPHECY	PASSAGE
To pay a temple tax Jesus prophesied to Peter that he would catch a fish with a coin in its mouth.	Matthew 17:24–27
Jesus prophesied that the temple would be destroyed within one generation. This took place in A.D. 70.	Matthew 23:1–2, 34; Mark 13:1–2; Luke 21:5–6
Jesus prophesied that the city of Jerusalem would be destroyed within one generation. This took place in A.D. 70.	Matthew 23:37–39; 24:3–20; Mark 13:5–22; Luke 19:41–44; 21:20–24
At the Last Supper Jesus prophesied that Peter would deny him three times before the next morning.	Matthew 26:34; Mark 14:30; Luke 22:34; John 13:38
As a prophet Jesus told his disciples that they would all fall away because of him that very night, "For it is written, 'I will strike the shepherd, and the sheep of the flock will be scattered.'"	Matthew 26:31; quoting Zechariah 13:7
Jesus prophesied his resurrection and said, "But after I am raised up, I will go before you to Galilee."	Matthew 26:32

Appendix 3: Prophecies Made by Jesus

PROPHECY	PASSAGE
Jesus prophesied the coming of the Holy Spirit.	John 14:16–17, 26; 15:26; 16:7, 13–15
Jesus prophesied when he told his disciples that shortly they would be filled with the Holy Spirit and with power and be witnesses to him. This has been fulfilled until the present.	Acts 1:8
Jesus prophesied his second coming, and that he would be the final judge.	Matthew 24:30–31, 36–43; 25:31–46; Mark 13:32–36; Luke 21:34–36
Jesus prophesied the final kingdom of God.	Matthew 19:28

Appendix 4:
Jesus's Seven Statements from the Cross

The Gospels record seven things Jesus said while being crucified.

From 9:00 o'clock until noon:

- STATEMENT #1: "Father, forgive them, for they know not what they do." (Luke 23:34)

- STATEMENT #2: To one of the thieves hanging by him he said, "Truly, I say to you, today you will be with me in paradise." (Luke 23:43)

- STATEMENT #3: In giving his disciple John the responsibility to care for his mother, Jesus said, "Behold, your mother!" (John 19:27)

About 3:00 o'clock p.m.:

- STATEMENT #4: "My God, my God, why have you forsaken me?" (Matthew 27:46; Mark 15:34)

- STATEMENT #5: "I am thirsty." (John 19:28)

- STATEMENT #6: "It is finished." (John 19:30)

- STATEMENT #7: "Father, into your hands I commit my spirit!" (Luke 23:46)

Additional Sources

Boettner, Loraine. *A Harmony of the Gospels*. Phillipsburg, NJ: P&R, 1976.

Kistemaker, Simon J. *The Miracles: Exploring the Mystery of Jesus's Divine Works*. Grand Rapids, MI: Baker, 2006.

———. *The Parables: Understanding the Stories Jesus Told*. Grand Rapids, MI: Baker, 2002.

Packer, J. I. *Concise Theology: A Guide to Historic Christian Beliefs*. Carol Stream, IL: Tyndale, 2001.

———. *Knowing God*. Downers Grove, IL: InterVarsity, 1993.

Robertson, O. Palmer. *Understanding the Land of the Bible*. Phillipsburg, NJ: P&R, 1966.

Smith, James E. *What the Bible Teaches About the Promised Messiah*. Nashville, TN: Thomas Nelson, 1993.

Sproul, R. C. *Essential Truths of the Christian Faith*. Carol Stream, IL: Tyndale, 1998.

———. *Saved From What?* Wheaton, IL: Crossway, 2002.

Scripture Index

1:6   *170*
1:8   *173, 203, 207*
1:9   *164, 203*
1:9–11   *176, 203*
1:10–11   *170, 203*
1:11   *187*
1:18   *108*
1:25   *108*
2:16–18   *xxi, 197*
2:24–28   *xxi, 197*
2:29–32   *152, 203*
2:32–36   *174, 203*
2:33   *173, 203*
2:37–47   *131, 201*
4:4   *131*
6:7   *131, 201*
12:17   *163*
14:11–15   *78*
15:3   *163*

Romans
1:3   *175*
1:4   *149*
3:23   *108, 194*
4:11   *10*
4:11–12   *60*
6:23   *94*
13:1–4   *32*

1 Corinthians
5:7   *95*
11:23–26   *94*
15:1–4   *193*
15:3–4   *78*
15:5   *165*
15:6   *162, 165*
15:7   *165*

15:17   *164*
15:22   *164*
15:26   *63*

2 Corinthians
5:8   *96*
5:21   *77*
13:1   *14*

Galatians
1:19   *163*

Ephesians
2:1   *96*
2:8–9   *145*

Philippians
1:23   *71*
3:20–21   *164, 177, 203*

Colossians
2:15   *34*

2 Thessalonians
1:6–10   *177, 203*

Titus
2:13   *77*

Hebrews
1:1–2   *76*
1:3   *77*
1:8   *77*
1:10   *77*
1:6   *78, 187*
2:14–15   *34*
2:14–16   *186*

Topical Index

virgin birth of, *xx*, *2, 3, 4, 7,
15, 23 ,184, 197*
Jewish leaders, *17, 46, 47, 49, 50,
51, 65, 84, 103, 104, 105, 112,
118, 119, 122, 131, 134, 141,
143, 149*
John (the apostle), *100, 106,
135, 136, 153, 161, 171, 209*
John the Baptist, *23, 24, 25, 26,
27, 39, 40, 63, 120, 184, 190,
195, 198*
Jonah, *150, 202*
Joseph of Arimathea, *143, 144*
Judas, *93, 94, 98, 103, 104, 105,
108, 122, 128, 156, 165, 188,
196*
judgment, *xviii, xix, 34, 78, 95,
101, 137, 178, 187*
judgment day, *34, 56, 57, 78,
199*
kingdom of God, *33, 78, 89,
164, 170, 199, 207*
Last Supper, the, *86, 91, 93, 94,
95, 106, 128, 137, 190, 195,
200, 206*
Lazarus, *40, 63, 64, 65, 66, 67,
68, 69, 83, 84, 85, 190, 195,
199*
love for God/Jesus, *1, 34,
87, 109, 161*
love for others, *161*
Magi, *15, 16, 17, 18, 19, 20, 190,
195, 198*
Mary (mother of Jesus), *xxiii, 3,
4, 5, 6, 7, 10, 11, 12, 13, 16,
17, 18, 19, 23, 136, 169, 184*
Mary Magdalene, *144, 153, 154,
164, 171*
Messiah, *xix, xx, xxiii, 5, 8, 11,
15, 17, 19, 24, 25, 26, 32, 39,
47, 49, 63, 64, 67, 78, 84, 85,
86, 87, 104, 114, 115, 179,
197, 198, 199, 200, 201, 202,
203*
Nicodemus, *143*

Passover, *91, 92, 93, 94, 95, 98,
103, 104, 121, 132, 141, 143,
173*
Paul (the apostle), *70, 77, 95, 96,
149, 177, 193, 203*
Pentecost, *151, 169, 172, 173,
174, 179, 190, 196, 203*
Peter (the apostle), *42, 95, 99,
100, 103, 105, 106, 107, 108,
109, 113, 128, 129, 151, 153,
161, 162, 165, 171, 172, 173,
174, 190, 196, 200, 206*
Pilate, *111, 113, 115, 117, 118,
119, 120, 121, 122, 123, 127,
129, 131, 142, 143*
praise, *9, 64, 85, 189*
prayer, *13, 68, 97, 98, 99, 100,
101, 102, 131, 190, 196, 200*
prophets
false, *xv, xvi, xvii, xviii*
foretelling, *xvii, xviii, xix, xx,
xxii, xxiii, xxiv, 3, 6, 13, 15,
17, 19, 23, 24, 25, 76, 95,
114, 151, 155, 157, 173, 179*
forthtelling, *xviii, 24, 76*
true, *xvi, xvii, xviii, xxii, xxiii,
xxiv*
providence. *See* God, providence
of.
ransom, *80, 81, 102, 137, 138,
202*
redemption, *13, 14, 32, 80, 81,
88, 124, 130, 138, 139, 154,
172*
repentance, *24, 25, 108, 130,
135, 145, 157*
resurrection of the body, *35, 63,
66, 69, 71, 141, 158, 164, 186*
right hand of God, *114, 172,
174, 175, 203*
sacrifice(s), *27, 28, 98, 140*
Sanhedrin, the, *111, 113, 115,
117, 118, 129, 141, 143*
Satan. *See* devil, the.
shepherds, *7, 175, 185, 195*

Topical Index

CPSIA information can be obtained
at www.ICGtesting.com
Printed in the USA
BVHW040339260121
598620BV00003B/6